MW01697507

Steve Kissell
and Eleven of his Comical Friends

HUMOR by the DOZEN

Dale Anderson
Joel Rutledge
Doyne Michie
Patty Wooten
Scott Friedman
Marianna Nunes
Louis Page
Ruth Hamilton
John Cooper
Frank Jeffreys
Bobbie Staten
Steve Kissell

illustrated by

Dom Rinaldo

Humor by the Dozen
© Copyright 1996, Steve Kissell
All rights reserved. No part of this publication may be reproduced or transmitted in any form. Reproduction of any kind is a really crummy thing to do.

Requests for permission to make copies of any part of the work or information on motivational seminars should be addressed to:

Steve Kissell
1227 Manchester Ave.
Norfolk, VA 23508
(757) 423-3867

Graphic Design: M.E. Witkowski,
One-Stop Publishing, Norfolk, VA

Second Edition

Table of Contents

Part I
Humor and Human Relations 5

Laughter: Life's Little Puffs of Pain 7
Bobbie Staten, RN, MPH

Humor and the "R" Thing 21
Marianna Nunes

Notes from a San Francisco Gumshoe 33
Joel Rutledge

Part II
Humor and Business 39

Teaming with Humor 41
Steve Kissell

Making Humor Work 65
Frank Jeffreys

A Funny Thing Happened
on the Way to the Sale 79
Scott Friedman

Part III
Humor and Kids 89

Humor in Education 91
Lou Page

The Laughing Parent 105
John Cooper

Part IV
Humor and Health 117

Therapeutic Uses of Humor 119
Ruth Hamilton

Laughter: Some Spiritual Aspects 129
Doyne E. Michie

Harnessing the Chemistry of Healing 139
Dale L. Anderson MD

Laughter and Healing 151
Patty Wooten

Part I

HUMOR and HUMAN RELATIONS

Bobbie Staten, RN, MPH, CSP

Bobbie Staten bases her presentations on a paradoxical foundation: graduate health degrees combined with a healthy and sometimes irreverent sense of humor about people and the lives they lead. In her witty way, she manages to have audiences laugh through topics of wellness, happiness, life and stress management, customer service, and people skills.

Bobbie's topics are from her personal battle with life, health, and finding happiness. For years Bobbie felt unfulfilled, working in careers that didn't especially match her talents or natural tendencies. She was unhappy, and it showed. She talks of turning life around and having the courage to take responsibility for finding one's own happiness.

Once a chronic dieter (the rhythm method of girth control), and an ex-two-pack-a-day smoker, she understands how hard it is to make lifestyle changes. However, first-hand knowledge provides her with a special insight that helps audiences find the courage to take the plunge! "Change what needs to be changed!"

Bobbie Staten, RN, MPH, CSP
3224 Green Level Rd. W.,
Apex, NC 27502 1-800-977-1144

1

Laughter: Life's Little Puffs of Pain

When people learn I started my career as a nurse, they are often puzzled as to how or why I switched from being a professional nurse to being a professional humorist. The answer is I didn't really switch; I just changed outfits and job titles. Enough of wearing that "wash-you-out" white from head to toe! Give me some color! Both occupations minister to your health, one through your body, the other through your emotions.

Humor has always been my answer to stress, pain, and anxiety. I grew up as an obese (fat) child and learned early on how to ease the pain and rejection I have always felt as a result of that through laughter. Anyone with physical defects (burns, limps, scars, etc.) will surely relate as we all have experienced the cruelty of childhood remarks on our differences.

All children want to be liked and praised. I wasn't particularly good in school, wasn't very athletic, wasn't attractive, but boy was I funny! People enjoy laughing and enjoy being around those who can make them laugh! Wow, such a simple statement, but it was my ticket to survival. And I quickly learned that if you can make fun of yourself before anyone else does, they will be laughing with you instead of at you!!! In nursing I discovered that laughter could not only ease my pain, but could ease the physical and emotional pain most folks feel in the hospital. So for as long as I can remember, I have looked for the humor in everyday events to ease the pain, the tension, and just the burden of living.

Mark Twain once said, "The secret of humor itself is not joy, but sorrow." We laugh at things we don't want to happen to us. For example, many jokes are based on someone falling down, getting a divorce, losing his money, etc. We laugh because we are relieved that it didn't happen to us! I call it letting out "little puffs of pain."

Another quote from Mark Twain reads, "In heaven there will be no laughter." I told my husband, "Well, if there is no laughter, I don't want to go!" He said, "Don't worry."

I tell that story in my presentations, and it always gets a laugh. One, because it is a typical example of a husband putting down a wife, and two, because we all have a subconscious anxiety about life after death. If there is a heaven and hell, we all know where we want to go!

Bad stuff happens to all of us. We do lose money; we do fall down; our health does decline; our spouses and jobs are not perfect, nor are our children (except my sister's). So how do we learn to cope? My answer is that we need to learn to laugh faster! You can suffer in silence and "waller" (done mainly in the South and much more exaggerated than traditional wallowing) in self-pity as long as you want, or you can go ahead and release that pain through laughter.

Humor is a disaster removed in time and put into proper perspective. People with a good sense of humor have learned to collapse the time between the hurt and the laugh. They have learned consciously to let go of pain by making fun of the thing that hurts, makes us angry, causes embarrassment or anxiety.

Take, for example, the episode of the "Driver's Permit Payback." My son had recently received his driver's permit but was still required to have an adult in the car while he was driving. (Reluctantly he agreed that I could qualify as the adult if I would promise to behave.) He asked me to let him drive by the school so that he could be seen by the guys. I agreed. Trust is such a naive thing.

The first two minutes went by smoothly. Steven backed up properly, did not hit the tree (this time) or the fence (now that we had rebuilt it), and managed to miss driving into the ditch at the driveway. I was so proud. We were going to be able to sell the Sherman tank after all. But then we reached the pavement and something frightening happened. My son, my previously relatively cooperative son, turned into someone else right before my eyes.

His whole demeanor changed, he became *a teenager*. He hung his elbow on the window sill; he slumped down in the seat, turned his baseball cap around on his head backwards. But then something even worse happened. He reached up with lightning speed and turned on the radio. That's right, punched in a FM heavy aluminum foil (or is that metal?) station and cranked the volume to a decibel level that would have been frowned upon by both OSHA and practicing audiologists "Steven!" I shrieked over the deafening noise, "Put both hands on the wheel and turn that radio down!" I just knew we were going to die. Where was his head? What had happened to that loving child of three minutes ago? "I'm driving," he hollered back. "Yea, but it's my

car," I countered having sunk to his level of arbitration skills. We were close to slugging it out as he repeatedly reached out to turn the music up and I reached up to turn it back down. The car was careening down the street making a good imitation of a huge boombox. My pulse throbbed to the beat. I was livid.

But suddenly, I realized that I am older and wiser than any teenager. So I sat back and lay in wait. (Readers, please smile here because, trust me, I was smiling at the time.)

I waited until he pulled up directly in front of the school, right beside the "in crowd," if you will, music blaring, windows down, and I broke out into the "Pony!" That's right, the classic dance of the 60's—arms, head, and hair 'a flying. He turned pale; I added an encore of the "swim." Guess how fast a motivated teenager can turn down a radio. The phrase "greased lightning" comes to mind. We don't drive together any more.

Now, I tell that story probably a little funnier than it actually was, but do you see how I used humor to defuse my anger? We both were able to laugh about it, maybe not that minute, but it has given us both a smile.

Laughter helps me get through the every day struggles of life. My husband Wayne worked as a finish carpenter for years. At the time of this writing, we are in our third year of an ongoing remodeling project in the 110–year–old farm house that we live in. My sisters comment that they don't know how I stand it, and let me know that they think I should probably "demand" that we complete the project. I guess that is one way I could handle it, but, honestly, most days I hardly even notice the mess. Some days I come home to find the floors of entire rooms missing. That's noticeable.

One day the kitchen cabinets were not where I had left them that morning. When it was time to cook supper, I noticed the cabinet that held the can goods wasn't hanging in its customary place. I asked calmly, "Wayne, where's the food?" The answer: "Down in the barn!" He had not bothered to empty the cabinets before he had moved them. It's hard to cook dinner without the food. A finish carpenter. An oxymoron. All I can do is laugh.

Some days Wayne helps me un-trash the house. See, when you are remodeling "in-situ", routine cleaning takes on a new dimension. It's not your basic cleaning; we're moving debris like concrete blocks, sheet rock, and water pipes. It's hard work, but Wayne is used to hard work and heavy lifting. Things that really tire me out are a breeze for him. But the first day I watched him help me vacuum, I just had to laugh. There was Wayne vacuuming the floor with the canister vacuum machine tucked under his armpit like a football. Men! What can I say? If you can't laugh at that mental picture, you have a severe humor deficit!

Some things take longer to laugh at than others. The wait time is usually directly proportional to the degree of pain or embarrassment. Once it took me fifteen years to laugh at something. Let me tell you the story.

My mother wasn't the best cook in the world. I think that's a fairly tactful way of putting it, just in case she ever reads this book. Anyhow, biscuits were especially hard for her, so after years of trying, she just gave up and we had "whomp biscuits". Now, for those of you who aren't familiar with that descriptive term, whomp biscuits are the pre-formed biscuit dough that come in tubes that you can open by putting a spoon in the crease as directed, or you can just "whomp" them on the corner of the counter and, surprise, they just pop out! Voilà! Whomp biscuits!

The reason biscuits were such an issue is that Daddy wanted biscuits with every meal; that's right, breakfast, lunch, and dinner. But the discovery of whomp biscuits did not fix the second problem that Mother had with cooking biscuits. See that word, "cooking"? Yep, that was the problem. Even given the pre-formed dough, Mother couldn't cook. She just seemed to burn everything. Dough-a-la-flambé.

Burned biscuits would just set my dad off. To say he had a quick temper is putting it mildly. We all scampered out of the way when Dad got mad. Nobody wanted to be in the path of his wrath, although, surprisingly, until that date he had never hit one of us. But he had a way of making you think he might. (As children, Mother had told us that the reason she gave us spankings and Daddy did not and the reason we should always do exactly as he said, was that he had such a temper that she was afraid he would kill us if he ever broke loose and got started (with a spanking). Now, I don't have a very good memory, but there are some things that you just don't forget. That was one of them. Yes sir, we girls stayed out of Daddy's way. When that man spoke, we jumped.

Well, this particular night the biscuits were burning. We knew because you could smell them. Dad yelled, "Quick, get the biscuits out; they're burning!" Guess who was the lucky one standing at the stove. In my haste I fumbled with the oven door. I dropped the potholder. I tried to grab the biscuits off the hot pan without burning myself. But the bottoms were sticking, and I was pulling the biscuits apart. "Get something flat!" Daddy yelled. I reached back and grabbed a fork–the nearest thing in reach, but the fork crumbled the biscuits' bottoms. "I told you to get something flat!" Daddy yelled, louder this time, as he jumped up and grabbed a spatula and popped me with it firmly on my bottom.

All three girls and Mother stood in shock. Daddy had done the dreaded thing. If Mother's advice had been correct, I knew what was coming next: I knew I was going to die.

He didn't kill me, though. That was the extent of his wrath. But did I think that was funny that day? It was such an awful moment that we as a family never mentioned it again. But one Christmas, long after I was an adult and Daddy had passed away, the whole family had gathered for Christmas dinner. Mom asked one of the grandchildren to get the biscuits out of the oven. As the child was reaching up for the oven door, I said, "If I were you, I'd get something flat!" All my sisters, Mother, and I broke out in laughter. No one had to be told the joke. The pain had stayed as an unwelcome, unmentioned visitor until I was finally, after fifteen years, able to let go of it through laughter.

Laughter can't change the bad things that happen in life, but it can lessen the stress we feel when those things do happen. When we make mistakes, we can't undo the things we did or take back things we wish we hadn't said, but letting go through laughter can start the healing process on its way.

The examples I have given are taken from my home life; however, laughter in the work place can help in the same way. I remember once I nearly killed a patient with a medication error. Not a pleasant memory. I beat myself up mentally for weeks. I moped around and felt quite sorry for myself. My coworkers had had enough. They decided it was time for me to move on. They staged an overdose on a fake patient using M&Ms as pills, and called me in to the room to "discover" the disaster. Of course I almost fainted and hollered for help. They all jumped out of the closets, and we all had a big laugh. It scared me to death, but I have to admit that it was funny. You have to let go of pain and remorse even if you make serious mistakes.

For years I struggled with my career choices. I couldn't decide what I wanted to do and was unhappy with each job I had held. Since I didn't know what was really bothering me, I blamed my unhappiness on the location, and as a result, I moved fifteen times in the first five years I was out of school. I say "I" moved, but more correctly, I was moved—by my dad. My nomadic lifestyle was not funny to him. One day when I was lamenting that I still didn't know what I wanted to do for a living, he suggested that I try out for the *Guinness Book of Records*. I asked, "For what?" He said he was sure I could win in the category of the

person that had moved the most. He said, "You're the only person I know whose furniture is wearing out from the bottom up!"

Much of my chipper attitude has come from my dad. He was almost always happy. He did have an explosive temper, but it lasted only as long as the explosion. Otherwise, he was always "up." I can remember many a time when one of us wasn't happy, and would be looking sad, Daddy would ask, "Who licked the red off your candy?" Or he would insist that we change our sour expressions with, "I want to see 'happy biscuits'," his term for smiling faces. At the time it would make us all so mad, but that was my first lesson on how you actively take charge and change your mood. To this day, when I find myself down, depressed, sad, or just generally miserable, I decide to put on a "happy biscuit" face, and it's not long before the smile is genuine.

Life is not perfect. The quote that "In heaven there will be no laughter" goes on "because in heaven there is no sorrow." Pain is a part of life on this earth, and laughter lets us release little puffs of pain. I encourage you to laugh faster. We haven't got much time left. Get Puffin!'

Marianna Nunes

Marianna Nunes is a keynote speaker who captivates, motivates, and educates her audiences nationwide.

At the lowest point in her life, Marianna was diagnosed with cancer. Her personal relationship and business fell apart, and she was forced to go into debt. However, through a long process of raising her self-esteem and using laughter as a healing source, Marianna succeeded in rebuilding both her life and her career.

Today, Marianna travels extensively, offering programs to Fortune 500 companies, hospitals, and universities across the country. Her corporate clients include: Chevron, Apple Computers, Hewlett Packard, and Texas Instruments.

Marianna is also well known for her popular singles program, *The Art of Flirting*, in which her compassionate humor and effervescent personality delight audiences. Marianna and her program have been featured in *Life* magazine.

2
Humor and the "R" Thing
"R" means relationships, silly!

Once upon a time not so long ago in a whimsical little village called Burlingame, where the eucalyptus trees grow strong and proud, lived a woman named Marianna the Portuguese. In this same little village lived a man named Frederick the Norwegian. Marianna the Portuguese and Frederick the Norwegian lived somewhat happy lives as single people. But as everyone knows, they could not live happily ever after because they were both "single." (Don't blame me. I don't make the rules. I just tell the story.)

One sunny day in Burlingame, Marianna (a happy-dappy woman), who was always trying to find her soul-mate, was reading the personal ads in the Burlingame *Gazette*, as she did every morning.

At this juncture in our story a little background information about Marianna the Portuguese would be helpful. Marianna, our heroine, answered seventy-four (this is not a misprint!!!) personal ads in the Burlingame *Gazette* in her quest to live happily ever after with the man of her dreams. (Warning: It is not recommended that you try this in your own home without consulting a professional therapist.)

Marianna dated nerds, Kurds, Turks, and jerks. She went out with guys who were overly sensitive (who cried all the time), guys who were underly sensitive (Marianna cried all the time), and guys whose porch lights were on, but nobody was home. Some men were not emotionally available; some men were commitment-phobic, and then there were those who sold Amway.

Being a woman, Marianna looked at all men as fixer-uppers, but years of intense therapy had taught her that when the rubber meets the road, expecting to fix a man and make him into something truly worthwhile is not healthy thinking. In fact, it is downright rotten. And as her therapist said so many times, "Marianna the Portuguese, what's going on with you that you want to change this man?" As much as she admired and trusted her therapist, sometimes Marianna just wanted to strangle her. But all that aside, she knew that there were fixer-uppers, and there were fixer-uppers; that she had learned time and time again from dating many men.

In going out with all these men, Marianna often thought that she would get sick to her stomach if it were not for "one thing" (Not to be confused with the "one thing" in *City Slickers*). And that "one thing" for Marianna was: Humor. Marianna was passionate about humor. And you don't date seventy-four men without gathering a virtual cornucopia of humorous anecdotes.

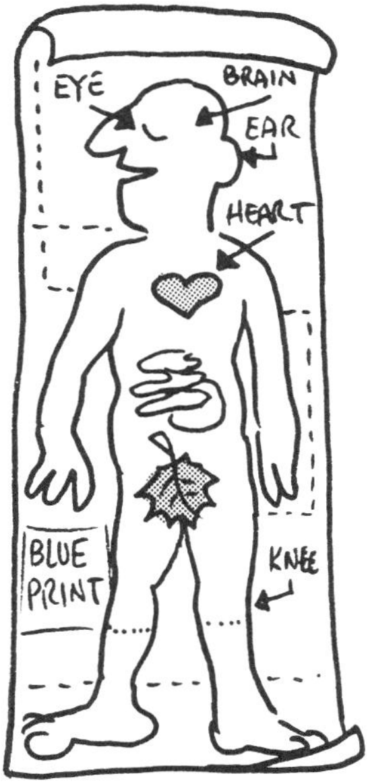

It has often been said that if Marianna was passionate about humor, she was "rolling in the hay" passionate about telling a humorous story on the phone, in her kitchen, or at the village market, bending the ear of anyone who would listen. For if a flower loves the bright sunshine and a gentle rain, Marianna loved an audience. Her two cats, Munchkin and Punam could attest to that. For many a lazy summer afternoon Marianna's furry friends sat attentively in the backyard amid the daises and the butterflies as their Portuguese mistress told them of her adventures in the strange and fantastic realm of personal ads.

At this point we shall return to our main story where Marianna the Portuguese is sitting in her kitchen reading the personal ads in the Burlingame *Gazette*, as she did every morning.

On this particular day, Marianna made a few quick, humorous (or perhaps not so humorous) notes in her diary about the date of the previous evening (number seventy-four to be exact). Putting down her diary, Marianna picked up the morning edition of the Burlingame *Gazette* and saw the following ad:

Breathing, has pulse, and can eat without assistance. If you chuckled, please call Frederick the Norwegian at 901-678-1234, Box 7383.

It is difficult to put into words what happened next. Marianna chuckled hysterically for seventeen minutes, interrupted only by thirty second intervals of torrential sobbing. Eventually, she turned beet red and fainted dead away.

Upon waking, our Portuguese heroine was all aflutter, partly because a dead faint can make you funny in the head, but, perhaps of greater importance, Marianna had a feeling in her body that she had found her soul-mate. Marianna giggled with delight because, as people in Northern California know, the body never lies.

But before she rose from the kitchen floor, Marianna noticed that the water vessel for Munchkin and Punam was as dry as a bone. Quickly she picked herself up and went to the

sink to fetch some fresh water, only to discover that the cloth angel that sat so long on the window sill had fallen into the sink. "Oh my heavens!" she exclaimed, barely able to contain herself, as she picked up the angel and held it tightly to her bosom. Surely this was the ultimate sign to Marianna that the man of her dreams was on his way. For not long ago her good friend Burt had given her some sagely advice about finding a soul-mate: "Just give it up to the angels, Marianna the Portuguese." That very day Marianna called Frederick the Norwegian, and they met for the first time; instantly, they knew that they were soul-mates.

Before we go any further, we must include a little background information on Frederick the Norwegian. To begin with, Frederick is what is commonly referred to as a gearhead, a man with vast stores of linear knowledge, as well as instinctive wisdom in the mysterious world of computers. Marianna, on the other hand, had never had a linear thought in her life. But not to worry, since Frederick was not looking for a gearhead like himself, but actually an old-fashioned woman to bring warmth and merriment into his logical life, not to mention a little hanky-panky. In some primitive way, Frederick the Norwegian realized that although a woman might be illogical as the day is long, he would find a deep soulful connection in a relationship with this spirited woman called Marianna the Portuguese.

Let us return to our main story, Marianna often passed the time with Frederick by telling him funny stories. Her exuberance in telling these tales was so great that she frequently forgot some crucial detail and left Frederick in the dark. Mildly confused and somewhat agitated, Frederick ferociously ferreted his way through Marianna's lack of logic to uncover a meaningful story, where initially there was none. As their relationship grew richer over time, Frederick discovered that decoding Marianna's "Portuguese logic" was actually a mysterious and exhilarating game to play. Once in a vulnerable moment, Marianna the Portuguese asked Frederick the Norwegian, "Do you think I should be less Portuguese and more logical?" And Frederick replied, "No Honey, that's just you."

As Marianna brought the illogical into Frederick's life, our Norwegian hero discovered his heart's desire in our Portuguese heroine, a woman who possessed a mystical way of relating to human beings and small-to-medium-size animals. As she walked upon the earth, her funny stories and merry heart inspired all who crossed her path. This is not to say that Marianna was perfect, for sometimes she could be quite the shrew. But alas, without a dark side, the light would not be so bright. And Frederick knew this since he himself was not without a shadow of his own.

Now they have been together for a year, well out of the glow period and deep into that place where even angels fear to tread—the human relationship. A realm of relating where human beings actually take off their pretty facades and get beyond the fuzzy-wuzzy projections of what they think the love of their life should be, down to the nitty-gritty of being really human, warts and all.

Let's get real quiet and see if we can hear what's going on as we drop in on Frederick, who is working in the garden, where he goes when stumped in the mysterious world of computers. Oh, and here comes Marianna looking for Frederick amid the petunias. Doesn't she look beautiful!

"Frederick, I'm looking for you amid the petunias. Where are you my big hunky Norwegian?"

Unfortunately for Marianna, Frederick is deep in linear thought, working out a pesky little bug in a software program that he has designed for an important client in Chicago. Frederick is working under a serious deadline with only one day left. So when merry Marianna walked into the garden with a nice fresh can of Coca Cola for her sweetie, an unfriendly growl was not what she expected.

Quickly she turned on her heels and scurried back to the kitchen, as she muttered, "Up your bucket Frederick the Norwegian, you stupid woodchuck!"

(This little unpleasantness is very embarrassing in a chapter on humor in relationships. But let's see what happens next.)

Marianna is sitting at the table reading "How to Live Happily with a Big, Hunky, but Sometimes–Grumpy Norwegian." She has already forgotten about Frederick's grumpiness. After seventeen years of therapy and 783 books on relationships, Marianna knew that when you want to live a happy life and there's grumpiness in the garden (and it's not you), then it's time to flow out of the garden and see the humor in the relationship. For as she often said in her colorful stories, there are three choices when you have a difficulty in life (especially in relationships): you can resist what's going on, be passive, or flow and see the humor in the situation.

Wait a minute! Frederick the Norwegian is coming out of the garden and heading for the kitchen, where Marianna the Portuguese sits at the kitchen table lost in her book. Frederick is smiling broadly with a deep sense of satisfaction. (He must have found the bug in the software.) But wait. Frederick has stuck a petunia in his right ear and a petunia in his left ear. Oh my, Frederick is such a kidder. (Frederick may be a linear kind of guy, but he surely knows the magic of humor in creating happy relationships.)

"Marianna, my love..." he says as he walks into the kitchen.

Marianna looks up at Frederick and just plain loses it. She giggles spasmodically with such delight that her cute little Portuguese head bobs up and down with laughter (like one of those little doggie heads in the back window of an automobile) so much that not a peep of sound was coming out of her mouth. It is quite a sight. Munchkin stops eating and turns his kitty head at an angle in disbelief. Punam runs out the back door and hides in the garbage can.

"Oh Frederick," Marianna finally exclaims with tears of joy in her eyes. "You are such a funny Norwegian with those petunias coming out of your ears."

"Marianna, I found the bug in my software. I didn't mean to growl at you. I was deep in linear thought. Some men go into their cave to work things out; I go into the garden. It's kind of a male thing."

"Oh Frederick, my hunky, linear, green-thumb Norwegian, I love you!"

Well, we must leave Frederick and Marianna and Munchkin and Punam, but let it always be known throughout the little village of Burlingame that Marianna the Portuguese and Frederick the Norwegian truly know how to nourish a happy relationship with an ample serving of humor.

Joel Rutledge

Joel Rutledge is a professional speaker/ humorist, writer, and stand-up comedian. He speaks in the U.S. and Canada on change, humor, and self esteem. His corporate clients include: Bechtel, Sprint, Hewlett-Packard, AT&T, and the United States Forest Service.

In 1990 Joel's comedy was broadcast nationally on CNN/TV. In 1993 he was nominated for the Twelfth Annual Communication Award by the National Council for Communication Disorders, for his work entitled "Good-bye to Mr. Normal," a compelling and humorous presentation on facing the challenge of being different. In 1993 Joel Rutledge was featured in the critically acclaimed documentary, "Able to Laugh," a film concerning the lives and humor of six comedians who have disabilities.

Mr. Rutledge is visually impaired and stuttered severely for the first twenty-five years of his life. He lives in San Francisco with his imaginary dog Spot. For further information, Joel Rutledge can be reached at: 415/753.1223; (f) 415/ 753.0337; Jo Rutledge@aol.com; 317 Judah St., San Francisco, CA 94122

3
Notes from a San Francisco Gumshoe

This is a true story. Only the names have been changed to protect the innocent.

San Francisco. You probably think Baghdad by the Bay is just one big wimp of a town, sporting that permissive postcard personality, with those pastel Victorian houses sitting high up on the hills gazing down upon those little cable cars that climb halfway to the stars.

But you're wrong. When the fog gets thick, this is a tough town, full of tough people who have the guts to leave the herd and find their own path. We're in touch with our feelings here, and we're not afraid to use them. We know where we stand, and it's not anywhere near a plate of Rice-A-Roni.

My name is Harper Hawkins, private eye, and I'm one tough gumshoe. And I've got the gumption to back it up. We're breaking out of this stiff and wooden literary genre and telling it like it is. Call me what you will, but don't call me late for cappuccino. I hate it when that happens.

I know what you're thinking. You want to know if I'm packing a .45 like Dirty Harry. Well, I'll tell you, smarty pants. I don't need a heater (not a radiator folks; a colloquialism meaning gun). And I don't pack a .45. I've got a disability. Actually I've got two of them. The most powerful weapons you can carry in America because a disability strikes at the very heart of the western psyche, the fear of being different, not fitting in, being a freak.

I guess you'd probably like to see my hardware. Well, I've got a high-powered, bilateral atrophe of the optic nerve. (I don't see too darn well.) And then, my own personal lethal weapon, which can rip apart the underpinnings of the fundamental structure of the rugged American Rorschach: An intermittent...unpredictable...hair trigger...speech impediment.

I didn't always carry my weapons so openly. In September of '52 my first-grade teacher, Mrs. Oglybee, put my desk smack-dab up against the blackboard because of my poor vision. The only problem was that I could feel the kids in the normal section looking at the back of my head, and I knew that they were thinking strange things about me. And the longer I sat there, the stranger I felt. I became obsessed with being normal.

And then they gave me those large-print books. I thought that "large" meant the print was large, and I suppose it was bigger than your regular print, but the books themselves were humongous. You could knock over a medium-size Buick with one of those things. So I did what any self-respecting kid would do. I took my large-print books home and stuck them under my bed. I used the regular books that the other kids used. At the age of six I was already involved in a secret, cover-up operation.

When I was seven, I started to stutter. Stuttering is embarrassing; it's humiliating. I felt like a freak. Every time I opened my mouth my self-esteem was on the line. When Joan Rivers said, "Can we talk?" I took it personally.

For years I blended into the fabric of society by keeping a low profile. I rarely opened my mouth. But deep down inside it was killing me. I knew that I was living a lie. Finally I just couldn't take it anymore. I had to face the fact that I was just a pretender.

But eleven years ago I stepped out of the shadows and walked into my own life. I guess you could say I was born again. Or if you were a Buddhist, you could say: This too shall pass.

I haven't always been this tough. When I first got into the detective business, I was gullible and took a lot of guff. But you see a lot of bad stuff in my kind of work that just makes you want to puke. I think that's why I have flashbacks now and then. Sometimes in the middle of the night I wake up in a cold sweat startled because I hear somebody screaming. And then I realize it's me.

My Jungian therapist says that it all goes back to the primordial swamp of my childhood, and that foggy day in March of '87, when somebody turned up dead, just touched it all off again. He could be right. But it's not an easy thing to live with, even if the chump deserved to die.

I used to lie awake at night and wonder why God made people who stuttered. Finally one night it occurred to me. It was so obvious. God made people who stuttered just to tick off those Type A personalities. You know the type. They're kind of impatient. A little stuttering can really slow them down. Have you ever seen a discussion between a Type A personality and a person who stutters? It's an ugly thing to watch.

But there was nobody watching on that foggy March morning, a little after six when I bumped into Bob at Sutter Street and Montgomery. And I still don't know what got into me. I've been pushed around by Type A personalities all my life, but somehow Bob just rubbed me the wrong way.

Blood was draining from his face as Bob waited for me to answer his question, as he realized that he could be completing fifteen to twenty things off his to-do list. And I'm intuitive. I felt his tension. But he made me feel so nervous. I started to talk even slower. And that's when Bob started to complete my sentences. Thirty-five years of rage rose up to the surface. I wondered how many people with speech impediments like myself had been destroyed by people like Bob.

And then I realized the real truth. Bob was politically incorrect. When he finished completing my sentence, I said, "Well Bob, that wasn't what I was really going to say." Even though it was—every...single...word. These people are never wrong.

But, for the first time in Bob's life, he thought he made a mistake. More blood was draining from his face. The entire bottom half of his body was shaking violently. In a desperate attempt to regain a sense of his self-worth, Bob lunged out hysterically one more time to complete my sentence. And I've got to tell you that it took everything I had, knowing that I was about to destroy the last remains of a highly-effective, well-oiled, smooth-running

Type A personality as I said, "Well Bob, that wasn't it either."

The coroner's report stated that Bob died of a massive stroke of unknown origin. The police took me down to the station for a few perfunctory questions and then let me go. As far as the authorities were concerned, his death was strictly a matter of poor health. But when the fog gets thick in the city, I always remember that desperate look in Bob's eyes when I said, "Well Bob, that wasn't it either."

Like I said, this is a tough town, full of tough people. And I used to think I was one of them, but now I'm not so sure.

Some people probably wonder why I do the work I do. It doesn't pay much, and every darn day eventually I want to say, "Take this job and shove it," but when my head hits the pillow at night, I always like to think that there's just a little more decency on this dirt bag of a planet we call home.

Part II

HUMOR and BUSINESS

Steve Kissell

Steve Kissell speaks nationally on humor can apply to our personal and professional life. Audiences learn to make positive changes in their attitude to reduce stress, promote team-building, and improve customer service. As a humorist, educator and motivational speaker, he has presented to such diverse groups as the FBI, the Dupont Corporation, 3M, and Aetna Life and Casualty.

After earning his Bachelor of Science in Education degree in 1987 (Magna cum laude) as well as the Elaine P. Whitty Scholarship for Educational Excellence, and a place in "Who's Who in American Colleges", he was an educator in the Norfolk (Virginia) Public School System and earned the School Bell Award for Teaching and Excellence.

Steve is the author of several books, including, *Surviving Life with Laughter* and *Never Take Comedy from a Stranger*. He is a member of the National Speakers Association, and serves as President of the Virginia Speakers Association.

4 Teaming with Humor

As part of our customer focus our office mails out a pre-program questionnaire. Pre-program means before the program. I don't mean to be condescending (that means talk down to you). The feedback we receive is used to design a program customized to fit the current climate and needs of the prospective company. In doing so we have discovered that many workers have the same concerns as their co-workers, or teammates (as I like to call them). I have discovered that different companies have many similar needs. In response to these common needs, I have developed a series of questions to be asked of each individual every day.

1. Are we a team?
   Do we work together each day? Are we sharing important information? Are you willing to give each customer personal service? Do you care about the customer or the money that the customer brings to your organization? Actually, team could be written as an acronym representing Together Everyone Achieves More. Though it may be trite, it's true that if we combine our talents and time, the workplace becomes more effective and more gratifying.

A story was told many years ago about a small village in a faraway time and place. The village elder was celebrating a birthday, and the decree went out that all the villagers should bring their favorite wine to the gathering place the night before the celebration and pour their best wine into a community container. On the night of the dance the village elder was to pull the cork from the container and all would share in the fruits of their labor (pardon the pun). The party was at its highest when the village elder withdrew the cork. To everyone's astonishment, only water flowed from the cask. You see, everyone had decided to save the best for themselves and placed only water in the barrel thinking that the others' efforts would hide their lack of effort. They deceived themselves as well as each other. We must do everything that we possibly can to give the best wine (not to be confused with whine) every day. Here are a few tips to enhance the team effort from day to day:

1. Help each other to be right, not wrong.
2. Look for ways to make new ideas work.
3. If in doubt, check it out! No assumptions!
4. Help each other to win.
5. Speak positively at every opportunity.
6. Maintain P.M.S. Positive Mental State
7. Act with initiative and courage.
8. Be enthusiastic. It's contagious!
9. Whatever you want, give it away!
10. Never give up!
11. Have fun!

2. Are you enthusiastic?
   Do you travel to work Monday morning at the same rate of speed that you go home on Friday afternoon? This is an excellent measurement of enthusiasm.

Some folks have made all kinds of excuses not to be enthusiastic. The one I hear most often is "I can't be enthusiastic; I've had a bad day!" With a comment like that I have no other recourse but to give them this assignment: Visit a local hospital. Go to the emergency room and pull back the curtain of one of the occupied rooms. Find someone there that has wires and tubes connected to their body and describe to them your bad day. If they look up at you and say, "You really have had a bad day!" you can complain.

Check out a local Wal-Mart or K-Mart. Who is the first person that you meet entering the store? You are welcomed by a greeter. Now that's enthusiasm!

Have you ever purchased Armoral? It's a goo that you put on the car vinyl. It makes it look brand new. Armoral employs only sixty-five people, yet supplies a product for the entire nation. Their per-employee profits each year are several million! How does a small company achieve this remarkable record? When asked, the CEO answered that the entire company acts as a team. Go figure!

Several years ago my wife and I went shopping for a minivan. We first looked at a Ford Astro. Oh sure, let's buy a car named after the Jetson's dog. I suppose it has an automated voice that says "It's wrainging. Activate the wrenshield wripers!" or "Rut row, out of gas!" We finally purchased a mini-van and were pleased as punch—until the radio quit working only a month later. When my wife took the car back, a new radio was installed, yet within a matter of days it too failed. After two more radio installations I was instructed by the boss (my wife) to call the dealership. I began the conversation on a positive note by telling the representative how much we enjoyed the van until the radio stopped working. He informed me that it was not the radio but the transistors in the radio. Thank goodness! He invited me to return the van and promised that in under thirty minutes they would have me back on the road with a working radio. I declined the invitation and informed him that we had returned the car four times for the same problem and that it was now the dealership's turn to reciprocate by visiting our home and making the necessary repairs. He explained to me that it was not their policy to make home visits. I then told him my policy was to give their dealership free advertising until they met my demands. This policy took the form of a citrus-shaped poster taped to the side of the car loudly declaring the name of the dealership. Each week I phoned the service department and they refused. Each time they refused I added an additional sign to the outside of the car. Eventually the car was literally covered in signs, which was no embarrassment to me since it was my wife's car! She finally convinced me to return the car. I was on my

way when my nine-year-old daughter, out of the blue, told me how proud she was of me for believing in what I was doing. Well, after that the car was definitely not going back. I decided on a more assertive action and phoned the owner of the dealership. I was routed to the service department instead. They recognized my name, realized I was holding for the owner, and finally relented. They came to our house that day and replaced the radio. Yes! The little guy finally won a round with big business. The story doesn't end there, though. Only a few months later it was time for me to purchase a car. Do you think that I went back to that dealership?

I visited a Honda dealership in a nearby town. The car is made in Ohio, my home state, and 85 percent of the parts are made in the good, old US of A. I purchased this Honda product, and what do you think happened three days later? No, the radio didn't fail, although that was a logical assumption (as Spock would say). The telephone rang. It was the Honda dealership wanting to know if I was enjoying my new car and informing me that they were sending me an evaluation. They inquired to see if I had any concerns before I even get the evaluation. What a difference between the two dealerships! One of these car dealers is proactive and the other, well, in the stone age I think. I believe that the minivan employees are still waiting for their bosses to ask them to be pro-active.

When an average consumer is satisfied with a product, they tell five to seven other people. If a consumer is unhappy, they may spread the news to ten to fifteen others. With me, I tend to tell over 20,000 people per year!

3. How well do you communicate? This question should probably be re-worded: How often do we mis-communicate?

Between correct gender language and the PC Police, America is inundated with constantly changing terminology. We must start speaking the same language. Here is an example: A SINGULAR SPECIMEN OF THE SCIENTIFIC CLASS OF AVIS CONTAINED WITHIN THE BOUNDARIES OF THE UPPER PREHENSILE ISEQUIVALENTLY VALUABLE AS A

DOUBLED INVENTORY OF THAT ITEM IN A LOW SPREADING THICKET. What did I just say? A bird in the hand is worth two in the bush!

The bottom line in communication skills is to listen carefully and attentively. Demonstrating that you are listening closely by repeating or rephrasing what the speaker has said helps to establish rapport. Even if you cannot help the speaker in any way with a problem, you will have given a wonderful gift just by listening. Here are a few thoughts on increasing our listening skills:

1. Listen effectively, while observing non-verbal messages.
2. Check the message by repeating what you heard.
3. Avoid communication blockers.
4. When the problem is clarified, encourage solutions.

We do however, need to be careful of listening too much. Check this out. One recent survey showed that the average employee spends more than three hundred hours a year listening to voice mail and responding to pages. This wasted time and effort not only costs companies $3 billion a year; it causes frustration for more than three out of four workers and stress for more than half. Worst of all, 45 percent of customers polled said that they took their business elsewhere when they couldn't get through.

Large advertisers of today listen to their consumers. Who doesn't like Cliff Clavin from Cheers? Remember the jovial postal worker who always had a surprising and interesting fact to share with everyone at the bar? Trigon of Blue Cross and Blue Shield wanted Americans to remember their name. They hired Cliff to tell the consumer just what the word Trigon really is: the former name of the Pentagon before they added two more sides and a Chinese food additive....M.S.T! The giant automaker Dodge has chosen a simple "Hi!" to say it all about their tiny, new car, the Neon. Coca-Cola has recently won awards in the advertising field by bombarding consumers with commercials of Polar bears talking about and drinking their product.

4. **Will all your customers receive quality service?** Let's do a little math for this one. 1+2+3=4. How does this work out? It's simple, if your employees are working together as a team, being enthusiastic and communicating well, then the customers that your organization serves cannot help but get quality service!

I couldn't decide on which of these definitions to share with you, so I hope you don't mind if I share both. Each is very exciting!

Quality service is satisfying the needs and requirements of the internal and external customer.

Quality is providing customers with products and services that consistently meet or exceed their needs, demands, requirements, or expectations at a price that represents value!

Whew! Those two are a mouthful and (as I promised) very exciting indeed. The bottom line of delivering quality service is that when all is said and done, you should have *done* more than you *said*!

Our local refuse department is very dedicated. Really! I know what you're thinking. This guy has too much time on his hands if he spends his free time observing folks pick up the garbage. Remember grasshopper: all that we do is observed. As I said, they are very dedicated. "How dedicated are they?" you ask. They are so dedicated that they refuse to throw away my garbage cans. That's right. I had one that had multiple holes and practically no bottom; both handles off! Do you think they would throw it away? Never! I left it out empty—they wouldn't take it. I put it in another can. They wouldn't take it. I smashed it down and put it in another can. They still wouldn't take it. In exasperation I left it out on the curb and placed a sign on it that read "THROW ME AWAY." They took the sign! Quality service, that's what I get, quality service!

5. Are you delighting the external customer?

An *external customer* is one who is serviced by your organization. It seems that these days we have lost sight of the little extra things that make our service memorable and different from other businesses in the field.

I deal with a small family-owned-and-operated printing company. It is close to our office, and the staff is friendly and efficient. Whenever I drop off an order on Monday, they promise that it will be ready by Thursday afternoon.

When Wednesday arrives, the phone rings. It's Best Printing with the ready order. How do they do this? It is simple. It's the technique of *under* promising and *over* delivering. They know that the order can be processed by Wednesday but they give themselves extra time in case there is a problem. There's nothing wrong with giving the client a pleasant surprise from time to time.

Situations arise that require me to visit a large home-and-business supply store. I won't mention the name just the initials—H.Q. Please don't get me wrong, H.Q. is Tim Allen's hangout and rightfully so; there's a lot of cool stuff there. Ever find a clerk to wait on you at a large store like this? Remember how they dart away to help someone for just a moment or to look for an item for you? How long does it take them? The next time you see them they are working at another large store with several more children to tell you about.

On the contrary, I love to shop at Meadowbrook Hardware in Norfolk, Virginia. Once again, it's in my neighborhood and the folks are really nice there. I know them all by name. Let's see there's Mr. Smith, T.J., and, uh, well a lot of other folks work there too. Not too many, though, because then it would become a really big place where the employees wander off into another dimension light years away. One day when I was a young newlywed stationed here, I sought refuge at this hardware store for advice and tool inventory. I bought a few things too many that day for what I had in my wallet. I discovered this fact at the register, with Mr. Smith looking on patiently. As I was about to put a few items back, he said, "I would be glad to put this on an account for you." I could hardly believe my ears. Here I was, a stranger, and he was extending credit to me. I felt like I was in Ike Godsey's store on Walton's Mountain. I grew to love this guy. Each visit he greets me at the door and accompanies me through the store with my list of needs. After hauling everything up to the counter, he charges everything to my wife's account (I love the man). Yes, I will undoubtedly pay more at this local hardware store, but their service is an added bonus. And it's worth it!

Have you ever noticed that it's only in the nicest hotels that they turn down your bed, phone you to check on your in-room food service, and make evaluations available to you? Perhaps they arrived at their present state by constantly improving.

5. Are you motivating internal customers?

An *internal customer*, of course, is one whom you work with on a daily basis. Can we really motivate the ones who share our workplace? I believe that we can excite and encourage them to motivate themselves. Let me give you an example. Once there was a couple who lived on a farm. Thanksgiving was approaching, and as in previous years they invited their children and their children's spouses to celebrate the holiday. Before the kids arrived, Mom insisted that Dad, who was hoping for grandchildren, not mention the

subject to their sons and daughters. She explained to him that today young couples actually plan a family and usually do other things first like traveling, building a home, or investing in a business. He promised not to inquire. Of course, he did have his fingers crossed at the time. The afternoon arrived, and Dad was called upon to say the blessing. He rose from his spot at the table and informed the family that he was truly blessed by the attendance of the children and their spouses filling the chairs around the table. "Of course, a few high chairs would be nice," he said. He also announced that he recently sold the last remaining farmland and opened a five-thousand-dollar trust fund for his first grandchild. With that he said a lengthy blessing. When he finished, he looked up, and his children were no longer at the table! I guess you might say that they were encouraged to motivate themselves.

To apply this principle to your office, begin a reward system for those employees who do outstanding work. Make it fun and enjoyable for everyone involved. An employee at Sentara Norfolk General Hospital came up with an inexpensive system of rewarding her coworkers at meetings. When her coworkers came up with a money-saving idea, she gave them *Pay Day* candy bars. If they completed a difficult project on time, she gave them *Crunch* Bars. If they implemented an idea and successfully gathered donations for a needy agency, she gave them *Rally* Bars. If they showed a sense of humor and boosted morale on the job, she rewarded them with a *Snickers* or an *Almond Joy* Bar. These investments cost between fifty and seventy-five cents (two dollars if you buy them at the movies). The point is that you really don't have to be the boss to reward another employee.

Of course, motivation can also encourage employees to diminish negative behavior. I recall one company that had a problem with several workers who were "punctually challenged." It seemed that they could not get to work on time. In response to the problem several of their supervisors conspired to come up with a solution. They wanted the solution to be easy and fun at the same time, so they decided to serenade the tardy suspects. They chose to play "Chariots of Fire" as the tardy employees arrived. From then on they arrived on time and ready to work. This technique boosted overall morale and increased profits.

I believe that there are two great truths about motivation.

1. If something feels good, people will usually keep doing it.
2. If it feels bad, after a while they will stop.

Amazingly, years of scientific study have been spent on this observation!

7. Do you participate in the ownership of your firm? Are you committed? Should you be committed?

There is a popular saying: Laugh and the whole world laughs with you; cry and you cry alone. I have added a stringer to this. Laugh alone and they put you away. Then you really are committed!

We should have ownership of our businesses. We own our churches and synagogues don't we? We raise money for a new bus, an addition to the building, or new office equipment. Likewise, we own the schools that our children attend. We are members of the PTA or PTO and raise money for new computers or to hire a new aide. Why shouldn't we feel as if we own our work? Some years ago, I observed an eccentric janitor at Lynhaven Mall in Virginia Beach, Virginia. He was nicknamed "Crazy Dave," and he provided shoppers with non-stop entertainment with his hilarious antics. Quite often you could find him mimicking a passing shopper, much to the delight of the onlookers. By the time a victim sensed someone following and turned around, he would be setting off in a new direction. If someone dropped a cigarette butt, he would whisk it in his dustpan with an unusual flair and pop it into the trash can. With that he would set out to dust the trashcan, squirt it with water and snap it a few times with his towel. He did everything with exaggeration and originality. Even his broom had become a rifle that he shouldered as he marched around the mall. Folks came from miles around to observe the wacky janitor; while they were there, they undoubtedly shopped. Do think that the managers of the stores or the owners of the mall minded his behavior? Do you think that they objected when *That's Incredible* and *Funniest Home Videos*, two national television shows, came to observe and tape him?

I know an elementary school principal in Norfolk, Virginia, who has students send him jokes and riddles for the school news program and the school newsletter. He is including the students in the running of the school as well as sharing humor. His name? Page, Lou Page (that's shaken, not stirred). If you bring a child to his school during the school year, he will without a doubt phone you that evening to see how your child's first day at school was. At the end of the week he will phone again and at the end of the first month as well. He has ownership of the school and is taking time out to include the parents as well. How many of us would love to get a *positive* call from our child's principal?

The other day I was watching a news program that featured an elementary-school bus driver in the South who dressed up as Elvis whenever he drove the children to school. The ensemble was complete with a white sequin outfit, black glasses, and large sideburns. He even had an eight-track stereo in the bus so that he could sing along with Elvis on his rounds. The reporter discovered that the students on his bus missed very few days. Why? Because Elvis was driving the bus! For all we know, it could have really been him!

8. Am I prepared for change?

It seems that almost every company that I work for mentions that they are undergoing change, as if they are the only ones. I believe that "change" has become a popular buzz word and that everyone is anxious to use it. Since time existed, we have all been changing and evolving. Companies are no exception; they are in a constant change mode.

Let me share with you a few observations that I have made about the wonder of change in business.

1. Change is inevitable; you cannot avoid it.
2. People look for and follow leaders during a period of change.
3. You must be moving to have change, much like a ship in the water, it must be moving to change course. Remember the old wooden ships with canvas sails? When the crew entered a storm, they would quite often toss over the side all non-essential gear in order to survive. Today, when a business enters a financial storm, it

invariably tosses over the side all non-essential gear. I hope that you are doing all that you can to be essential!

4. All change may not represent progress, but without change there can be no progress.
5. The future is not what you think it will be. It will hold many surprises for us. Check this out: More than twenty-five years ago, in the elation following the *Apollo* moon landing, America's premier airline announced it was accepting reservations for the first commercial flight to the moon. Takeoff was scheduled for the year 2000. Ronald Reagan was among those who immediately booked a seat. The name of the airline? Pan Am. The moral of the story? Grand plans are great. But the future unfolds one day, one decision at a time. And if you can't change, can't adapt along the way, you'll never reach your ultimate destination. Let's not forget what Yogi Berra said: "I may be lost, but I am certainly making good time!"
6. You need to maintain your sense of direction. Albert Einstein found himself on a train one day and being checked by the conductor. Al looked all over his coat and pockets and could not find the train ticket. The conductor assured him that he trusted him, and if Albert Einstein said he bought a ticket, then he did. Later the conductor passed Al once again, and this time he was down on the floor looking under all the seats. The conductor once again assured him that he trusted him and he did not have to produce the ticket. Albert was frazzled; he told the conductor that it was

not a matter of trust, but of direction; he didn't know where he was going!

7. Final question: Do you have any sense of humor? Everyone has a sense of humor, but what I am asking of you is do you have any sense about humor? I believe that we all have it, and if you hear someone say differently, please poke them in the eye! We really need to examine ourselves and discover the elf in yourself! We should laugh as much as we can, especially at work. I do believe that we can laugh at work and still keep our jobs! Humor is important because people are important. Humor makes every situation more human, we are the only animal on earth that laughs. Well, maybe flipper if you want to count a dolphin.

In a poll by Hodge-Cronin of 1,000 bosses, 98 percent said they preferred hiring an applicant with a good sense of humor; 84 percent believed that people with a sense of humor would do a better job. Please remember these golden stars of humor in the workplace:

1. People like to hire people with a sense of humor.
2. The cheapest benefit of any job is laughter.
3. If fun is allowed, people will want to come to work!

With all that said I would like to close this lengthy chapter with a story that will sum up the nine points of "lite" of humor as a team builder. There was once a village wise man who was approached by a teenager. The young man had captured a small bird and had it hidden in his hands behind his back. He told the wise man that he had a bird behind his back, and then he asked him: "Is it alive or dead?" The boy knew that if the wiseman said that it was dead, then the boy would simply release the bird proving him wrong. If he guessed that it was alive, then he would simply crush the bird and display it dead; either way the old man would be made a fool. The old man did not answer right away; he thought for a moment and answered with this, "The answer is in your hands." What a cool answer! And so I say the answers to these nine questions are in your hands as well.

Remember how I mentioned that I wanted to close this chapter with one story? I lied. I have one more. Would you like to hear about it? It's a sequel to the story above. You see, the bird was released and it flew off into the winter sky. Sad to say, it began to rain, and the water struck the wings of the flying bird. It turned to ice (wing de-icers had not been invented yet). Losing power, the bird crashed to the earth in a field, and it knew instinctively that it could not survive the cold winter night. Just as it was about to perish, a cow wandered by and dropped a cow pie right on top of the bird! Under normal circumstances this would be bad; however, now the bird was warm and protected from the elements. It was so happy that it popped out it's little head and began to sing with glee. Suddenly, a cat appeared, heard the singing bird and ate the bird. What moral could arise from this story? Not one moral could be found, not two not four, but three morals!

Number 1: It is not necessarily all the bad people that can put you in a pile of manure.

Number 2: It is not always good people who can rescue you from tragedy.

Number 3: Most importantly, if you should find yourself in a pile of doo-doo, don't sing about it!

Frank Jeffreys

Frank Jeffreys "retired" from the world of science and academia as physics instructor at a women's college to live his dream of writing and acting in 1983. Since then he's "worked as much as any actor I know," appearing in five feature films in 1995, two of which played at the Sundance Festival in 1996, one with Sir Anthony Hopkins, and even a George Lucas film. He has written two full movie screenplays and one stage play with several in process at this time. He has also written scores of inspirational, motivational, and/or humorous articles for organizations and magazines. Currently, he is working on a series that is a humorous look at the single male life and a group of nostalgic stories from the South. Even before any of the above accolades, "the day I quit working my life away and started living my dream I was a success. From there things just keep getting better and better." Life is a win-win game that can be as big as we dream.

5 Making Humor Work

You're asleep. The alarm goes off. You leave the sweet embrace of sleep, get out of bed, and go to your regular nine to five. Where's the fun in that?

You might start by asking yourself the question, "Do I want to be the greatest asset I can be to my company or just get it over with?" If you just want to get it over with, it's time for you to get out of your rut and re-evaluate your life. Someone once said that a rut is just a string of coffins with the ends knocked out. If you want to stay in your rut, you probably wouldn't be reading this, so I'll assume all of you with regular jobs want to be on that upward spiral of success and gratification.

If you want to be the greatest asset to your company, humor will figure prominently. Every moment of our lives (on the job included) we make a decision to be either a center of negativity, hate, aggression, and stress or a center for "positivity", love, acceptance, and laughter. It's easy to see which category would be the greatest asset to your workplace. Employers and employees alike are realizing that the old, dour, stuffed-shirt image of the professional was never the most productive. The office joker, however, is not usually the most productive either.

The new professional image is seen as someone who is secure enough to not mind if people see their human side, which includes mistakes, emotions, and humor. Humor puts colleagues at ease, restores perspective, and engenders the creativity needed to solve problems in new ways. As Joel Goodman puts it: "People who don't laugh at work fall into tunnel vision. They are not as open to creative solutions." Humor also helps us smooth out the lumps of failure, which, if you are working up to your potential, is bound to happen.

O.K., so now that you're at work, what do you do to liven up the place? Nothing. Most likely, your manager is perfectly happy just the way

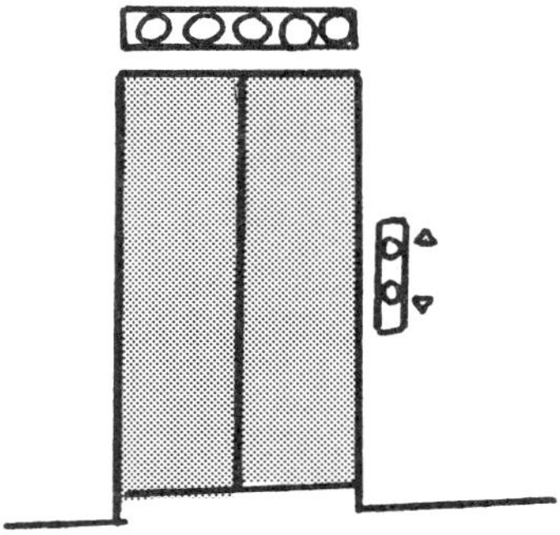

things are. If you are the manager, your employees will probably appreciate your not rocking the boat too much right now. There is almost always resistance to change, even when it is needed. Besides, if you go around putting rubber noses on everyone and hitting people on the head with a foam hammer, you are sure to make all involved extremely uncomfortable...including yourself.

Your first mission, should you decide to accept it, is to become intimately acquainted—no, not with the boss's first eligible offspring—with your own sense of humor. Look for humor on the job. Notice the double entendres, the literal meaning of work-related phrases and abbreviations; be aggressive in your search to find what you think is funny. Start a journal not only of what you find funny on the job, but also what you find funny elsewhere. Begin a collection of work-related cartoons, and start your company's own humor history. Get to know your unique sense of humor. If you think it's funny, it's a good bet that a lot of other people will think it's funny too. Once you have gotten a firm grasp on your funny bone, it's time to look for humor outlets in the workplace.

Does your office have a place to go to laugh and joke and just relax? How can your break room be lightened up to engender lighthearted discussion? How can the prevailing attitude at meetings be changed for the better? Does your company offer "mental health days" like sick days when you just feel too good to go to work? How can you help fellow employees gain perspective? What can you do to accept, redirect, and affirm an

angry, aggressive verbal attack?

Tomorrow morning when you get up, make faces at yourself in the mirror, make funny noises, start a humorous routine that gets you going on the light side. Get that humorless log out of your own eye before you complain about the speck in someone else's. Plan to put humor in your day; don't just rely on luck. Remember to carry your humor journal with you until you have a good foundation of humorous anecdotes.

Once you've found all the places where you can add a little humor, slowly start softening up the resistance to change. It is truly remarkable what can happen. Often, just letting people know it's O.K. to laugh is enough. Some big corporations actually have paid mental health days. Others have laughing rooms or bulletin boards. Some encourage jokes and laugh sessions before brainstorming meetings. All have found a rise in productivity, improved attitudes, increases in creativity, lower stress levels, and greater motivation among their employees. Be sensitive to the needs of the company and your fellow employees; when it's right, you'll know it.

Humor may be helpful in memos and reminders, to defuse anger, as a relief from stress and to put clients at ease. It may also be used to increase motivation or help to build rapport among clients. One of the most powerful uses for humor recognized as far back as Galileo's time is to aid in policy and behavioral changes. More on that topic later. One of the best references I have found that gives a real nuts-and-bolts description of implementing on-the-job humor is "Making

Humor Work" by Terry L. Paulson, Ph.D. This work/funbook gives you activities and axioms to help you insert humor into your life and workplace.

Making My Business Your Business

OK. You're asleep. The alarm doesn't go off because you just crawled into bed at 4:30 A.M. after driving home from a humor presentation across the state. You're not about to get up until nature calls. When it calls about quarter of nine, you're up and running.

So it's not running off to work, but you do have a deadline on that article you have to write, business to drum up, and rehearsals, always rehearsals. The dishes have been piling up for a week because you haven't had time away from the word processor in days. Between bursts of writing, you field calls from leads you have thrown out, sometimes months ago. At least two friends call you from work because they are bored, want to talk to someone, and know you're not "working" so you get the lucky ring. You remember it's Tuesday, so you have to rush to a lesson—voice, acting, gymnastics, whatever. On the way home you remember it's the third Tuesday of the month, so it's off to another professional meeting, one which, like many others, you sit astride of and must attend to keep up with news in that field.

Add to the above a reasonable workout time, quiet time, personal time, meal time, social time, wife, husband, or significant-other time, and TIME OUT! There aren't that many hours in a day. No one would work like this for anyone *unless* you're self-employed and willing to take this job and love it.

We each make decisions as to what kind of life we will lead. Some feel that working for someone else, often being unhappy, unfulfilled, and frustrated is just the way the world works. Only the lucky ones have landed a job that they truly enjoy. Well, that's not the way it has to be, and in truth most of the world does not operate that way. What if you actually went out and started doing what you have always—in your heart of hearts—wanted to do?

I often tell people I stopped working in 1983, my last year as physics instructor at a private women's college, and I don't ever intend to work again. In all my working life, this is the first time I have ever experienced true abundance. A whole lot more than just my basic needs have been met even though I have not had that regular paycheck every month. I realized if I don't do what I want to do NOW, when am I going to do it? Life for me instantly became a joy, not a job.

Many people still do not know what they really want to do with their lives, what to be when they grow up. Others know but are afraid to admit it for fear of failure or being laughed at. Even as a kid, I knew what I really wanted to do: write and perform. Through that medium I can bring joy and positive changes into people's lives. Humor presenter fits in well with these goals. Being a humor presenter allows me to make a real impact on the quality of people's lives by validating the use of humor for everyone. This is similar to the proverbial "give a man a fish or teach a man to fish." Tell someone a joke, and they may laugh a while. Let someone know that it's O.K. for them to be funny, and they can laugh for a lifetime.

I have already mentioned that if you think it's funny, there's a good chance others will think it's funny, too. There is however, a large percentage of the population who are humorphobics—afraid to tell a joke or even to try to be funny. Stumbling over punch lines and bungling jokes is humorous in

itself. If your listeners have any sense of humor at all they can figure out how the joke should have been told and still enjoy it. In addition, they can laugh with you at the telling of it because we have all been in similar situations. Keeping the light of laughter from someone's life simply because it may make you feel somewhat uncomfortable is extremely selfish and harmfully egocentric.

The need for humor in industry is legion. Industry needs humor presenters who can validate the use of humor to help the system. Then it needs humorists who can make the employees laugh and learn. The most real kind of humor comes from on the job. Interview employees and find out what's really going on behind the scenes. A good handle on the fundamentals behind the processes used by the company and being at ease with proper lab technique are helpful, too.

From whatever angle you attack the challenge, you will find you can never know too much or research too long. Being realistic, I usually give myself only two or three weeks for this phase, including writing and rehearsing the lines. Finally, since you are presenting for people in the field, you should be prepared to show some expertise in several areas then give them a show that they couldn't do themselves. This is one of the reasons I include so much physical comedy and stunt work in my show. I've never had an audience member say "Shucks, I could'a done that!" I *have* heard comments like, "Say, don't you work on the third shift?" from employees who are sure that I also work there. That closeness to the real thing is just what you want.

Every issue has a funny side. Even such topics as death, unemployment, and sickness can be dealt with humorously. We proved that in our "Laughter, Loss, and Healing" workshop last year. Large corporations, who are about the only clients you find who can afford to hire someone outside the company for a few weeks, are usually more uptight about changes than anyone else. They are concerned that the changes are understood and implemented by everyone and are willing to go to some extra expense to have those changes quickly understood and adhered to. Enter humor. A quick look at the masters of changing behavior and belief systems can be helpful.

Gallileo Galilei was known for his obstinacy and argumentativeness as a young man, but it was his wit and charm that won him influential friends in Venice when he was at the university at Padua. His humor and perspective also most assuredly kept him from being executed during the Inquisition. Even when he was forced to swear that he believed in the Copernican system of astronomy in which the stars and planets orbit around a motionless earth, Galileo was quoted as saying under his breath after each recitation, 'Eppur si muove" (But it does move!).

One of the lessons of Galileo that I find most useful is his method of getting his radical new discoveries out to the people through role-playing. Galileo's short, humorous plays were performed out on the streets and usually involved three performers, Sagredio, Salvatius, and Simplicio. Sagredio stood for the business and church community, Salvatius, an open-minded but wise man who exposed the new concept through experimentation, and Simplicio, the fool or common man. When by the end of the play, Simplicio understands the new concept (as does the entire audience), it would be embarrassing for the clergy to admit that they cannot accept what even a fool can see is true. In my corporate safety shows, I often use my sad clown character, Slim Chance, as Simplicio, a happy clown for Salvatius, and the audience for Sagredio.

Galileo's plays were written with many layers, double entendres, and puns. Simplicio, for example, stood not only for the fool but also for the fact that the Truth is simple, *and* for Simplicius, a major proponent of Aristotle, whom Galileo was openly contradicting. Simplicio often directly quoted the edicts handed down from the Pope thereby showing his faulty logic. Galileo was a master at showing the logical contradictions in a certain way of thinking, setting up a definitive test, then bowling the people over with his conclusion—just the way a good joke should be told.

From Galileo to Darwin to Einstein many of the great moments in changing the world view have been done with humor. That Darwin was seasick for the seven years during the voyage of the *Beagle* while he was gathering his information about evolution and could still keep his tongue-in-cheek perspective is a monumental tribute to anyone's sense of humor. Albert Einstein is another giant whose wit and humor are well known. And you thought that this humor bandwagon just got rolling recently!

From these few examples, it can be seen that humor and creativity go hand in hand. Any attempt at levity should be viewed as a grand endeavor, not a demeaning one. Mohammed in the Koran even said, "He deserves Paradise who makes his companions laugh." The types of humor that don't work, ethnic, sarcastic, unrelated to the job, embarrassing, crass, or profane make themselves quickly evident. It only hurts when you laugh—at me.

Scott Friedman

A motivational humorist, Scott Friedman gets your audience laughing...and skillfully slips in plenty of practical ideas on overcoming stress, conquering burnout and making change work. While tickling funny bones with a quick wit and playful style, Scott is opening minds to new ideas. Participants leave feeling better about themselves, their careers, and their futures.

Scott holds a degree in marketing and psychology from Southern Methodist University. Scott twice served as president of the Colorado Speakers Association and earned the Certified Speaking Professional designation from the National Speakers Association.

Phone: (303) 671-7222;
e-mail: FunnyScott@aol.com;
internet:http://www.scott-friedman.com;
mail: Scott Friedman, CSP
1563 South Trenton Court
Denver, CO 80231-2617.

6

A Funny Thing Happened on the Way to the Sale

As uncertainty and anxiety in the business world reach epidemic proportions, people are searching for a new prescription to stay competitive, or at least sane! Humor is the perfect remedy! Humor has now been scientifically proven to relieve stress, improve productivity, motivate workers *and increase sales*!

A woman attending one of my seminars confirmed the power of humor. She said she used to worry about her son Brian. Brian didn't seem to fit in at school. Some days he came home from school crying because he didn't think he was liked by the other kids. Then one day everything changed! Brian raced home from school and proudly proclaimed that he had found the secret to making friends. "Just make them laugh," he beamed, "and they will like you!"

The same "secret" applies to sales of any sort. Successful selling is actually about making friends. The best salespeople seem to have a special knack for building rapport. By contrast, those who fail to do so generate just the opposite results. Have you ever gone out to buy something, found exactly what you wanted, but decided against buying it because you didn't like the salesperson? A salesperson has the power to make *or break* the sale. It's really as simple as little Brian's axiom to make people laugh and they will like you. People buy from people they like. And they like people who make them laugh. Humor and laughter create instant rapport and camaraderie among people; they enhance receptivity and reduce resistance; they help establish a bond between people on which a relationship can be built. So once you get people laughing, you've laid the groundwork for doing business with them.

Good salespeople make the entire sales process fun. When they communicate, they touch not only the minds of their prospects, but their hearts and funny bones as well! It is important not to confuse a salesperson with a comedian. A comedian succeeds just by being funny, but a salesperson succeeds only when the humor helps to sell the product or service, or build customer loyalty.

People often say they envy those who are funny and able to make others laugh. But anyone can learn to be more humorous with a little effort and practice. Humor is a learned skill, like playing the guitar. It begins with cultivating an appreciation of humor whenever and wherever you find it and then making the effort to incorporate humor rituals into your daily life, particularly your daily sales routine. Not every attempt will come off as you'd hoped, but the ultimate payoff for those who keep trying is increased commissions. You are limited only by your imagination. Here are a few ideas to start your creative humor wheels turning toward improved business relationships and increased sales:

1. Write humorous notes on the outside of your letters, such as: "Please open before reading!" "Danger: Contents of letter may make you smile!" "Warning: Enclosed proposal has been proven to make large sums of money for laboratory rats."

Engaging your prospects "in fun" may increase their receptivity to your proposal.

2. Include cartoons in your correspondence to clients.

Most people love cartoons. If you send product information, don't be afraid to include a personalized cartoon that targets your service or product. People will identify with positive, witty, and friendly characters. Your characters can poke "gentle" fun at a familiar situation. A good cartoon won't say it all, but it invites people to pay attention to what you have to say.

3. Use incongruity when handling objections: "All right! So you don't like the contract! Okay, I'll paint it green!" By breaking the tension, incongruity gives you the opportunity to regain control of the situation.

4. Use calculated self-effacing humor to help alleviate misunderstandings.

When dealing with an angry person, resist the temptation to react on the same level and fight back. Instead, use humor to defuse the tension. Should an irate client ask, "Do you suffer from insanity?" your response could be, "No, I enjoy it!" Or if a client walks in and says, "Okay, who is the idiot in charge here?" you could say, "I'm head idiot; how can we solve this challenge?"

Such an unexpected response absorbs and redirects anger in a harmless way without putting the other person down. Even if you are unable to control the attitudes or behavior of those around you, you can always keep your sense of humor and control your reaction to their anger.

5. Poke fun at yourself and people will laugh with you, not at you.

Tell personal stories where the lesson is learned at your expense. It will make you appear more human, more vulnerable, more approachable—an instant rapport builder.

Self-effacing humor is so effective that it ranks as a leadership trait. It reflects strength and confidence. It shows that you are secure enough to laugh at yourself. It also creates instant rapport, defuses tension, and makes you more likable. Refrain from making off-color or derogatory remarks about others. Trying to draw laughs at the expense of others shows a lack of good sense, compassion, and professionalism.

True humor has its roots in kindness and affection. The highest form of humor is to laugh at yourself; the lowest form is to laugh at someone else.

6. Be unique in dealing with your clients.

Send a fork with a note saying, "I'm hungry for your business!" How about a mini-service station with a greasy note attached saying, "Best Service in Town." Send your message on top of a cake. You may just find doing business becomes a piece of cake! People will even forgive a few bad puns when they know your intent is to amuse them. Try sending your message via telegram to a client. Or get really wild and hire a singing telegram company to convey your message in verse.

Salespeople are using humor-studded tactics to get through to the hardest-to-sell prospects. One made a prospect the beneficiary of a huge sum of flight insurance, available at all airports. On the policy she wrote, "My last thoughts were of you." Another woman removes the arm of a doll and sends it to an elusive prospect with the message, "I'd give my right arm to see you!"

To get meetings off to a productive and positive start, serve everyone ice cream or suckers. There's something very humorous and warming about sitting around a table with three people with blue tongues.

Practice "rehearsed spontaneity." In dealing with clients, we have certain situations that seem to come up again and again. You can anticipate such situations and be ready with a fresh, well-rehearsed, "spontaneous" response. To the objection, "The price of this house is just too high!" you might reply, "Well, if we took out the kitchen we could save you about $6,000." To the question, "How long will it take to get the product shipped?" you could

answer, "Oh, about eighteen months to two years, but once you get it, you're going to love it!" (Suddenly, fourteen weeks doesn't seem so long!) Or you could ask, "Do you know the difference between my becoming your primary supplier, and a Caesar salad?" "No? Then how about having lunch on Tuesday."

The artful use of humor tends to relax prospects; in that state, they become more open, more likely to tell you things they wouldn't normally reveal, so you gain the inside track on how to meet their real needs. It uncovers hidden objections and moves the client closer to "Yes!" A tense or uncomfortable prospect is far less willing to have an open discussion with you or reveal any real problems or concerns.

Even if you are selling the best product or service in the world, you increase your advantage if you incorporate just enough humor to break up the monotony and keep the prospect interested. You can't reason with someone who isn't paying attention!. Many a prospect has walked away from a sale out of sheer boredom. Humor attracts and holds attention. It appeals to a sense of enjoyment rather than a sense of logic.

One of the hottest places to develop new clients and stay in touch with existing ones is through the Internet. Because it is such a new medium, it is still a very personal way to stay in touch. It's sort of like belonging to a private club! People tend to respond to e-mail messages more quickly and reliably than to phone messages or snail mail! Because it fosters a kind of playfulness, sharing positive, appropriate humor via e-mail can create an immediate bond. The World Wide Web has many sites from which to find this kind of clean, appropriate humor. Log on; go "surfing," and start sharing the wave of humor!

Will humor work with every sale? Nothing works all the time, but ask yourself: does it work with you? Most people love a good laugh and are receptive to humor. Sometimes you just have to pay close attention to find their funny bones!

Every situation is unique. Each interaction with other people requires you to assess the situation from a fresh perspective. You must recognize individual nuances, make adjustments, and use good judgment. Common sense is a prerequisite for using humor successfully.

But, humor will never substitute for effective salesmanship. You must still know your product, be able to solve client problems, and be persistent in your follow-up. Humor will then give you the sales advantage because, remember, you're not in the "sales" business; you're in the "people" business. Humor is a technique that can be learned, practiced, and developed, just like other skills. Try it!

Discover for yourself that those who chuckle have more fun *and laugh all the way to the bank*!

Part III

HUMOR and KIDS

Lou Page

Lou Page has been an educator in the Norfolk Public Schools for close to twenty-five years. He began his career as a Kindergarten teacher and now serves as an elementary school principal.

Each day, he is conscious of his ability to touch hundreds of lives—students, parents, and teachers.

7
Humor in Education

What's the least humorous way to start an article on humor in education?

Probably by looking up the definition in the dictionary.

Here it is anyway, according to Webster:

Education—The process of training and developing the knowledge, skill, mind, character, etc.

This definition implies that even if you are not involved in a traditional classroom situation, you are an educator if you participate in training, instruction, teaching, cultivating, or nurturing in any form and the information in this article will be useful to you.

Education is a difficult job. All day, teachers stand in front of kids, many of whom don't want to be there. Then after a hard day of teaching they go home and grade papers all night. Day after day they do it all over again. Perhaps that explains why the comedian Gallagher reflects that the home-economics teachers are divorced, the coaches are fat, and the shop teachers are missing fingers. What do you expect in a situation like that?

Whether your workplace is a school building or a downtown office, workplace climate can be defined simply as "the way people feel when they're at work." Many factors affect the workplace environment. In a school, many different relationships exist: teacher–student, administrator–student, parent–teacher, administrator–teacher, and so forth. Things can get complicated because interpersonal relationships are complex. For example, if a teacher fights with his spouse, it may affect his administrator, the other teachers, and the students. When the students are having problems, it probably affects the parents, and they may involve the administration.

Is it any wonder that teaching is considered one of the most stressful professions? For example, one of my teachers was a recent college graduate. As the school year progressed, she faced many of the situations described above. She began to develop ulcers, so under her doctor's recommendation, she asked for a leave of absence. Surprisingly, she chose to visit a Latin–American country, which, at the time, was going through a lot of turmoil. We didn't hear from her for two or three months, but then this letter arrived.

Dear Faculty,

I've got good news and bad news. The bad news is that on the way to my vacation, the plane was hijacked, and it was flown to a little grass strip out in the middle of this country, and a guerrilla leader commandeered me. My life has really changed. All day long I spend my time dodging snipers taking potshots at me and driving trucks full of explosives across minefields. It's really different.

The good news is my ulcers have cleared up!

Yes, human interactions are difficult. How can humor help improve these relationships? Research shows that a significant relationship exists between human factors, the school climate, and leadership style. Since leadership style is the salient factor that influences productivity and satisfaction of individuals in the workplace, leaders have good reason to develop humor skills. I want to address two questions to help leaders incorporate humor in the workplace.

1. How can leaders use humor to increase their effectiveness?
2. When should leaders use humor?

Using humor to increase effectiveness

The goals of a school, like those of any organization can be defined on a continuum. At one end of the continuum are the needs of the individual, at the other, the needs of the organization. Ideally, all of our goals should be oriented towards the individuals in the organization, because organizations only exist to serve people. In this scenario, we might ask the question "What can we do to make our employees feel great about work?" We could provide them with a great health–care plan, liberal retirement benefits, stock options, and shorter working hours. However, if we concentrate *solely* on the individual the organization may suffer. There's a good chance that if we focus only on human needs and wants the organization will not achieve its goals. In business the bottom line will be the profit margin; in an educational setting the bottom line is student achievement. At the other end of the continuum we could concentrate solely on the needs of the organization. We could reduce the number of employees, lengthen work hours, and eliminate employee benefits. In the short run we could increase the profit margin. However, we won't be able to keep employees, because they won't want to work in this type of climate. So in the long run, the business will suffer.

Of course, the key is to find a balance. With a balanced approach, both the needs of the individual and the needs of the organization can be met. People will be happy, and they will enjoy coming to work. The organization will have good employee productivity, optimal employee health, more profits, and test scores will rise. Humor can help us achieve the balance.

How can humor help achieve the balance? First of all, humor strengthens interpersonal relationships. It provides perspective, insight, and gives focus to feelings. Take for example the following observation.

Many people view life as a donut. To some it's rich and enjoyable; to others, it's as empty as the hole. To the pessimist, the optimist seems foolish. Who's really foolish, the one looking at the donut or the one looking at the hole?

This anecdote provides insight into pessimism and optimism and a unique picture of the end result of each.

Humor can also neutralize negative emotions. In any place where adults interact, occasionally you will have negative emotions. Communication will come to a standstill. Humor can break these impasses and build a sense of spirit and camaraderie among employees. It facilitates communication, lessens hostility, and creates a relaxed atmosphere where people can work together and get things done.

When Should Teachers Use Humor?

There are some times when humor is not appropriate. Like a scalpel, in the hands of one who uses it skillfully, humor can do a lot of good. Used incorrectly it can do great damage.

Let me give you an example from my day–to–day experience. Let's say two children get into a fight. Of course one is the winner; the other now knows he should have followed the school rules. The winner enters my office saying "Well, I had to fight, man; he was talkin' about my momma. I can't let him talk about my momma like that, so I punched him." This is a great opportunity to use humor and teach a valuable lesson. Usually I ask him to "Tell me that I have a big, fat nose." He is usually not willing to do this for fear that I'm going to suspend him. Finally, I'll make him say it; first softly, then louder, until he's yelling "Mr. Page, you have a big, fat nose." About that time, a smile comes on his face because I do have a big fat nose. Then I reinforce a lesson "I could get really mad because you said I have a big, fat nose, or I can choose to ignore it. I don't have to hit you because you said I have a big fat nose." Then I can talk to him about the need to think things through before reacting because the use of humor moved the student from a defensive posture and encouraged an open attitude that was receptive to the point I was making.

The other student provides the perfect example of when *not* to use humor. He's hurt, crying, and he's not ready for someone to use humor. He will perceive humor as making light of the situation. So be careful. If a person comes to you with a serious problem it's probably not a good time to use humor.

Secondly, keep humor within the bounds of your position. It's more appropriate to use humor with a subordinate than with a supervisor. However, if your supervisor has a good sense of humor and the two of you have a good relationship, a humorous comment might be appreciated, but you must be sensitive to the situation.

A third time that you shouldn't use humor is when you are giving a presentation to a hostile audience. They want you to make a mistake. You need to win a hostile audience over *before* you attempt to use humor. If you can't win them over, don't try jokes. They will only make the situation worse.

A final difficult time to use humor is when you are a part of a larger presentation. For example, if in the middle of a budget presentation you are asked to present your department's budget, humor probably won't work if it is incongruent with the tone of the rest of the presentation.

Humor and Thinking Skills

Humor requires complex thinking. That's why some jokes that are funny to adults are not funny to children.

When thinking about using humor with children, you have to be aware of the concept of the "experiential map." For example, if a child grows up in the city, surrounded by sky-scrapers, the child will not be able to understand or relate to the phrase "under the spreading chestnut tree." There is no mental picture, no internalized concept of a chestnut tree with which the child can relate.

A popular Will Roger's line is "When Congress makes a law, it's a joke, and when they make a joke it's a law." Adults can relate to this joke because they have experience with committees and they understand the legislative process. Children don't understand this line because they have no experiences in that area.

The other thing humor requires is a differing point of view. You have to be able to look at things two different ways. Piaget, the educational psychologist, tells us that children have to be in the formal-operational stage for that to happen, and that starts at about age twelve. Children under the age of twelve find it difficult to understand verbal humor. They need a mental picture. That's why children's entertainers use slapstick. It's the most visual type of humor. Only use verbal humor with students when it creates a vivid picture in their mind.

Once students reach age twelve they can start understanding more sophisticated types of humor. At that point your opportunities to use humor in the classroom expand.

For example, when you're talking about how important it is to write clearly, you could bring in real examples of headlines that don't communicate as intended. Some examples are:

"Food is basic to student diet"
"Dog runs wild. Bites several people in the north end"
"Blue skies unless cloudy"
"War dims hope for peace"
"Slipping and falling in tubs is often due to curved bottoms"

Children can appreciate these once they are the proper age. These help them to understand the importance of writing clearly.

Keep your eyes open for things that make your classroom a little more fun. A good source of humor in the classroom is comedy classics such as the books by Shel Silverstein.

Rudy Flesh knows how to belch better than anyone ever did.
Margo says that Rudy Flesh is a nasty, vulgar kid.
Some day he will go to Hell or jail or Canada, but now
Every night I pray that first Rudy Flesh will show me how.

Make good use of cartoons. Include humorous questions among the serious ones. "What convinces you that Henry VIII had eight wives? Was it worth it? Or you could put in the directions: "Be sure to write on at least one side of the paper." You can also teach children other types of humor related to word play, for example:

Spoonerisms: I like to keep my icicles well boiled.
Daffynitions: Aftermath—that which follows arithmetic.
Tom Swifties: "You struck oil," she gushed.

By teaching these traditional types of humor we are actually developing thinking skills. The structure of humor usually involves one of these devices: metaphor, analogy, simile, comparison, contrast, or cause and effect. When children understand and write humor, the use of these literary devices uses thinking skills on the highest levels, including analysis, synthesis, and evaluation.

In summary, recognize that schools and other

organizations are places where human beings live, work, and play. Education is not only preparation for life; it is life itself. The people involved in that process must be able to laugh, cry, be angry or elated. All of us make mistakes, say silly things, get confused, misuse words, give stupid answers, forget to zip our zippers. We have to be able to laugh at ourselves.

John Cooper

John Cooper is creative energetic, and outrageous! Whether he's speaking to a group of parents at PTA or talking to a group of CEO's, they're always having fun. John teaches people how to add more fun and creativity to their personal and professional lives. His twenty-six-year background in the variety arts makes John's presentations lively and unique.

John is a graduate (Thank the Lordy) of the School of Hard Knocks. He's married to a wonderful wife (Catherine), and he is the proud father of a fifteen-year-old son (John).

For more information on John and his fun and unique programs call (404) 363-9230 or write: John Cooper, 762 South Ave., Forest Park, GA 30050.

8
The Laughing Parent

One hundred years from now,
It won't matter what car I drove,
What kind of house I lived in,
How much I had in my bank account,
Nor what my clothes looked like;
But, the world may be a little better
Because I was important in the life of a child.
--Unknown

Below are some suggestions to help you make family time memorable. Remember: add the word TOGETHER to all of them. Keep in touch with your children so they will stay in touch with you.

Ways to Say "I Love You"

Hug, kiss, pat, stroke hair, pat cheeks, scratch backs. Touch speaks when words can't.

Give your child a wallet with your picture inside, so they can know you're always with them.

Talk about when they were little and how much you wanted them.

If your child arrives home first be sure there is a snack and welcoming note.

Make meals a time to talk rather than watch television.

Go to your child's school and have lunch with them once a month.

Leave notes where your child can find them when you're not there. Share warm thoughts that suggest your presence even when you're gone.

On Father's Day or Mother's Day send them a card of thanks for the honor of being their parent.

Play "hooky" from work and school together. Enjoy the day by doing things that you wouldn't do on a normal day off.

Show up for games, performances, and all the important events in your child's life.

Making Fun Family Memories

Lunch Box Surprises—Put a note or funny drawing on the napkin in your child's lunch box. Once a month put in an extra dessert.

Use sidewalk chalk to design a family masterpiece. Let the rain wash it away.

Once a month send a surprise to your child through the mail (stick of gum, funny card, sticker, etc.)

Once a month have desserts only for supper.

Walk around the block. Make up funny stories about the pets in the neighborhood.

Count Your Blessings—Have a candlelight dinner, complete with flowers on the table. Have each member of the family tell what they are thankful for and why.

A great question to ask: "What good things happened to you today?"

In winter have an indoor picnic. Have hot dogs, potato chips, sodas, paper plates, etc.

Birthday Bash—Wake your child up singing Happy Birthday. Crown him or her king or queen for the day. Hide small surprises around the house for a birthday treasure hunt.

On family vacations send home postcards to your children. Sign them, "Having a great time, glad you're here!"

Always exchange "Hello" and "Goodbye" kisses with your children.

Draw funny pictures.

Grow a plant or plant a garden.

Share a hot fudge sundae.

Make a funny family video, adding to it yearly.

Buy some face paints and paint each others' faces. Yes, let them paint your face too.

Toss the baseball or football now and then.

Take your child out on a date. One-on-one quality time is very important. Let your child pick the restaurant and movie.

Ask your child to help select your clothing for the next day. Limit them to 2 selections and be sure to wear them.

Have a tickling match. Let your child win.

Tell your child about the day they were born.

Let your child help you wash your car. It's a wonderfully messy job for a young child.

Roast marshmallows over a campfire.

Pan for gold.

Hunt for four-leaf clovers. Share the luck.

Play "I Spy."

Watch a sunrise and sunset.

Teach your child a new word.

Make ice cream sodas.

Play pick up sticks.

Camp out in your living room.

Play jacks.

Mail your child a funny card.

Play balloon basketball; use a waste paper basket for a hoop.

Make sock puppets, put on a show.

Learn to count in a foreign language.

Tape record your child reading or telling a favorite story.

Tell your child they have a beautiful smile.

Have a sock war; 5 minutes, 20 pairs of socks.

Have a tea party.

Play dress up.

Roast marshmallows over a candle.

Share a favorite childhood story.

Put flowers in your child's room.

Play bingo.

Collect comics, sports cards, etc.

Give your child a bear hug.

Make your own funny papers. Have copies made and sent to grandparents, aunts, uncles, and friends.

Visit your local library.

Serve your child breakfast in bed.

Set family goals together.

Order brochures from the Department of Tourism. Dream a vacation together.

Play charades.

Play "Pin the Tail on the Donkey."

Teach your child to blow a bubble-gum bubble.

Enjoy an old-fashioned hayride.

Build something using blocks.

Teach your child how to play spoons.

Have an indoor scavenger hunt.

Have a silly-face contest. Be sure to take pictures for this year's holiday cards.

Blow bubbles.

Do a jigsaw puzzle.

Bake cookies.

Praise Your Child

Outstanding
You're incredible
I'm proud of you
Phenomenal
You're wonderful
What a good listener
I trust you
Bravo
Spectacular
Hip, hip, hooray
Very creative
You're a winner
Remarkable
You're important
Excellent
Fantastic
Super job
Awesome
Marvelous
Beautiful
Well done

Jest For Laughs

Why do birds fly south?
Because its too far to walk.

Why did the hippopotamus cross the road?
Because it was the chicken's day off.

What kind of building has over 10,000 stories?
The library.

What color is the wind?
Blew.

What do you get when you cross a pogo stick and a cow?
A milkshake.

What side of a cat has the most fur?
The outside.

Why did the girl blush when she opened the refrigerator?
She saw the salad dressing.

Why do elephants have trunks?
Because they'd look funny with glove compartments.

What part of the fish weighs the most?
The scales.

Why did the elephant sit on the marshmallow?
To keep from falling in the hot chocolate.

Roses are red,
Roses are yellow;
Grandfather's teeth
Are lost in the Jell-O.

What can you take that you can never give back?
A bath.

Neat Places to Visit with Your Children

Airports
Amusement parks
Animal Shelters
Arcades
Art Gallery
Art Supply Store
Book Store
Botanical Garden
Craft Store
Farmer's Market
Fire Station
Fish Hatchery
Governor's
Mansion
Historical
Cemetery
Historical
Landmark
Hobby Shop
Hotel
Humane Society
Library
Nature Park
Pet Store
Petting Zoo
Planetarium
Police Station
Railroad
Museum
Science
Museum
Shopping Mall
Toy Store
Zoo

Remember: it's not how much money you spend on your children, but how much time. Now, go make some family memories.

I Am a Parent

I am a parent.
I have been given the gift of a child.
It is my opportunity to help this child find their path in the world.
I am a protector, provider, teacher, mentor, encourager, esteem-builder, supporter, storyteller, confidant, coach, playmate, friend, finder of lost treasures, trailblazer, and dream weaver.
I give the gifts of love, understanding, laughter, patience, guidance, self-responsibility, and encouragement.
I receive the gifts of love, admiration, trust, respect, laughter, understanding, playfulness, and youth.
I am a warrior fighting daily fear, ignorance, prejudice, apathy, hate, and low self-esteem.
I have a past rich with memories: the first word, the first laugh, the first smile, the first accomplishment.
I have a rewarding future filled with hope, love, expectation, adventure, and fun.
I touch and mold the future.
I am a parent.

Part IV

Humor and Health

Ruth Hamilton

Ruth Hamilton is Executive Director of Carolina Health & Humor Association, a nonprofit organization dedicated to promoting humor in health care, in business, and in the community. She founded Carolina Ha Ha in 1986 and has continued since then to develop humor systems which instill light-hearted programming in businesses and health care facilities. A national speaker on Empowering Humor Systems, Ruth enjoys helping everyone find their own "funny bone." Certified Humor Presenter is a speakers' training which she offers to everyone who wants to put more laughter and group interaction into their professional presentations. For the corporate sector, Ruth developed Energy Resources Training which concentrates on building positive communication and stress management skills. For a decade, she has published "The Carolina Ha Ha," a monthly newsletter that features humor options for a world that sometimes forgets to laugh. Laughter, applied humor, and community action are Ruth's avenues for combating apathy and instilling positive change. Contact Ruth Hamilton at (919) 544-2370 or the web site http://repnet.org/~cahaha.

9
Therapeutic Uses of Humor

Humor is a perspective that enables one to view stress and pain with a softer edge. Though not an immediate cure for trauma, chronic illness, or emotional stress, humor can be a therapeutic tool. It offers positive outlets for chronically ill patients and also for stressed-out medical and corporate staff. For many years medical workers have recognized that patients with a positive mental attitude and shared laughter respond better to treatment. Physiological responses to laughter include increased respiration, circulation, hormonal and digestive enzyme secretion, and a leveling of blood pressure. Many report a general sense of euphoria after vigorous laughter. But until the *New England Journal of Medicine* published the Norman Cousins case study, few considered the therapeutic uses of humor. The first documented case of humor's positively affecting disease was in 1964 when Norman Cousins published *Anatomy of an Illness*. Medical professionals were for the first time shown that humor biologically reversed Cousins' *ankylosing spondylitis*, a painful disease causing the disintegration of the spinal connective tissue. Given a one-in-five-hundred chance of recovery, Cousins decided to infuse himself with humor treatments. With Cousins' self-designed humor treatments, he documented that fifteen minutes of hearty laughter could produce two hours of pain-free sleep. Blood samples also showed that his inflammation level was lowered after the humor treatments. Eventually Cousins was able completely to reverse the illness. Following the example of Cousins, many health-care facilities as well as corporations have established humor programs as an aid to patient/employee health.

Carolina Health and Humor Association (Carolina Ha Ha), incorporated in 1986, is an educational service foundation specializing in humor programing for health care and personal growth. I founded the nonprofit and continue to serve as Executive Director. An early program included the Laugh Mobile and was developed for Duke University Medical Center in 1987 by Carolina Ha Ha. This became the Duke Humor Project and offers bedside humor interventions to cancer patients. Coordinated with Duke's department of Oncology Recreation Therapy, patients get humorous interactions that invite them to use the media on the Laugh Mobile. This rolling display cart with a circus motif delivers a wide variety of humorous media, including books, audio and video tapes, games, and clowning props. Patients are invited to use their hospital time to learn a new skill that will increase creativity and keep the mind active. Distraction becomes a resource for pain

management. Boredom is fought through positive experiences.

The framework for humor interventions is a plan to promote joy and laughter in patients which offers may positive effects in their recovery. Humor volunteers may engage in yo-yo demonstrations, guitar-playing, or just friendly banter that reveals clues to patient humor preferences. Water guns may be dispensed to allow the patient to fight back during the rigorous oncology treatment. Patient assessments document the effectiveness of the humor intervention and offer the recreation staff and volunteers continuity of interventions. I have assisted dozens of hospitals nationwide in implementing humor programs patterned after the Duke Humor Project. The Laugh Mobile is also manufactured by Carolina Ha Ha and has been sold nationally. Medical staffs report that Laugh Mobile programs build morale and emphasize the value of a sense of humor.

During my nine years as a volunteer humor therapist for the Duke Oncology unit, I have had many experiences that showed me that humor is at hand even when situations seem humorless. One that sticks in my mind is when I wheeled the Laugh Mobile into a business executive's room, complete with laptop computer and fax. I announced to the somewhat annoyed patient that I was his humor therapist and that now it was time to laugh a little. "And how do you expect me to laugh when I'm behind schedule?" I was somewhat amused for he was hooked up to an intravenous chemotherapy pole and had on his executive pajamas. His secretary wife stepped aside as I took charge of the treatment. Quickly I showed him the Wee-Waterful. This is a push-button game filled with water in which basketball is played. With the push of the button, a bubble of air propels a little basketball into a miniature goal. The executive patient was vaguely interested but asked, "And what are the rules to this game?" "Mister, this game doesn't have any rules; it's just for fun!" Well, I managed to get him to try this game and to tell him about the importance of laughter for the immune system. As I turned to leave, his wife followed me out of the room. She pulled me aside and said, "Honey, you're the first woman in twenty years who has shut him up."

The next time I visited him, I asked him about the Wee-Waterful basketball game. He said he enjoyed it after he figured out what the rules were going to be. It's all in a day's play for me when I can trick someone into having fun by suggesting a game has no rules.

Another time I visited the oncology unit with my friend Kathy who has a giant rabbit puppet named Harriet. We were visiting the rooms when a lady had a streak of brilliance. She suggested that we put Harriet the four-foot rabbit in the bed, and the lady could hide in the bathroom. She activated the call button just as we were gone on our way. I wish I could have seen the nurse when she checked on the rabbit tucked in the bed.

Practical jokes have always been a favorite part of my therapy with patients. Another time I was passing out whoopee cushions and instructing on the proper use. One gentleman decided he would hide it under the covers and ask the doctor to sit on the bed when he made rounds. He even practiced how he would motion for the poor tired doc to take a load off his feet and sit a spell. I was anxious to find out how this prank had turned out when I went back the next week. The playful gent reported that he tried faithfully for a week to get the docs to sit on the bed on the whoopee cushion, and not one would try. But wouldn't you know it: every nurse he called in was more than happy to take part in the prank and activate the whoopee cushion.

Sometimes the simplest little toys can change a whole floor into a place of laughter. On this day, I was passing out yo-yo's to the patients and encouraging them to practice a "totally useless skill." I knew I had a winner when I gave the yo-yo to this energetic six-ish lad. His blue eyes lit up and a big smile took over his face. He instantly became the "Yo-yo Man of 9100."

The past ten years have flown by, and I've loved every moment of my volunteer position as humor therapist for Duke oncology unit. It's always been the little sustaining chuckles that keep me coming back, but it's a rare patient who wants all the humor I can dish their way. One such patient was a lovely lady who always requested that I come before she started her pain medicine so that she would be alert. On this particular visit, my friend was relaying how itchy her head was now that all her hair was falling out. She was worrying that she would drive her husband mad scratching all weekend. I told her about exaggeration and the Gorilla routine. She caught on fast and improvised a skit of a gorilla scratching wildly while waving his lanky arms around. We all had a big laugh, and I knew she would use this humor treatment. She later told me that this was just the trick that got her through the weekend. She didn't say how her business-like husband received her wild antics.

There is no joy greater than laughing with cancer patients because they quickly become your friends. Often I'm laughing through tears, for I'm not sure if these patients will be around when I come back the next week. But I have so many happy memories of the Yo-Yo Man of 9100 and the Gorilla Lady that my humor cornucopia overflows. I'm blessed to have found a way to serve that feeds my soul, heart, and mind. Should you ever think that there isn't much to laugh about, follow me on my rounds with the Laugh Mobile, and I'll show you a down-right good time.

Doyne E. Michie

Doyne began to be interested in laughter therapy when, during visits to friends in military hospitals in World War II, he realized that some kind of added dynamic was present beyond the "friendly enjoyment" normal to such situations. The therapeutic aspects of laughter became more and more evident during pastoral experiences in hospitals and nursing homes, where the sensitive use of humor and laughter proved itself in situations from short-term hospitalizations through serious problems.

He has presented Laughter Therapy Workshops for the national convention of the American College of Chaplains, hospitals across the country, including Johns Hopkins Hospital in Baltimore, Medical Societies in several states, Hospice groups, Area and National Church Conferences, and many large corporations such as A.T.&T., Southern Bell, and Coca-Cola Co.

For more information about Doyne's presentations, contact him at either 404-256-1077 or 1-800-256-LAFF. His mail address is: 616 Lorell Terrace, Atlanta, Georgia 30328.

10 Laughter: Some Spiritual Aspects

"A merry heart doeth good, like a medicine."
Prov. 7:22 (KJV)

There is a pretty heavy quote that I don't know to whom to attribute but it has intrigued me for a long time: "God is a comedian playing for an audience that's afraid to laugh."

If you agree that man (excuse me, ladies: "homo sapiens") is the only animal that laughs, and that the Bible assures us that we are made in God's image, then that heavy quote should intrigue us.

After all, what is at the heart of our humanity?

Those of us who have seen so many times how our sense of humor has helped deal with some of life's rawest experiences come close to feeling that our sense of humor just may be at the heart of our humanity.

Those of us willing to explore evolution have heard more than once that the emergence of an "opposable thumb" was a significant step in developing Homo Sapiens. But we aren't the only animal (putting things in biological terms) with an opposable thumb.

Some say "man" is "a tool-making animal," but TV's Discovery Channel aficionados have seen lots of nature-study programs showing

animals using "tools." A chimpanzee pushing a stick down a termite hole, resulting in a feast of termites, hardly compares to a computer, but a stick is a tool.

"Man" can "communicate." But, again, we know that other animals "communicate." We are getting more and more impressed with the sophistication of the dolphins' "clicking language," but I can't believe that one dolphin edges another aside and says, "Have you heard the one about the three tunas and the ruptured porpoise...?"

"Man" is the only animal that laughs, and our sense of humor just may be at the heart of our humanity. Advertisers have long sensed that. Many advertising campaigns have been built on humor because agencies long ago discovered that if they can grab your sense of humor, "they go'cha," and can sell you their product. You haven't heard this for years, but all of you can finish this famous slogan: "I can't believe I ate..." For years that approach sold a lot of Alka-Seltzer.

All this begins to speak to me as I reflect on my experiences in bringing the therapy of laughter to Hospice patients—by specific invitation, in individual cases, of the two Hospice groups with which I volunteer.

As I presume you know, Hospice support can be invited only after a doctor, in his/her professional opinion, has indicated that a loved one has six months or less to live. All Hospice patients *know* themselves to be dying; and it's nearly always painfully obvious. Cancer patients are wan and emaciated from their months or years of struggling with that ravaging disease. Advanced diabetics have usually lost one or more of their limbs, sometimes a few inches at a time. A ten-year-old boy for whom we put together a great (and final) birthday party had a massive brain tumor visible on the side of his head. I cite these unpleasant facts only to make the point that for *years*, in most cases, the experiences of these patients have been de-humanizing. Hospitals provide needed and welcome lifesaving services, for which many

of us have personal reasons to be grateful, but they pretty much have to "do it their way," and little of it is fun. They take away your clothes, feed you on their schedule, do procedures when *they* choose. Unavoidably, to one degree or another, this is de-humanizing, and little of all this changes during those last six months of these Hospice patients' lives.

And then someone comes in for a half hour with the therapy of laughter. I do it with the comedy I have built into the "close up" (one-on-one) magic tricks I have honed through years of use. When invited to visit Hospice patients I don't "announce" that I am there to give them a dose of the therapy of laughter. And as I leave, I don't point out that I've just "zapped" them with some laughter therapy. I just go in and "have fun with them" for half an hour. (The magic tricks I find effective involve a lot of touching. I ask for their hand; they give it to me, and "something funny" happens in that hand. There is a dimension and dynamic in all that touching which could make another chapter of this book. It's Victor Borge's astute observation "that a laugh is the shortest distance between two people.")

I never verbalize any of these concepts or dynamics to these patients, but what I have come to understand is that indirectly, through laughter, I am simply reaffirming their humanity. In a subtle way I am communicating to that terminally ill patient, "You have had (usually) years of de-humanizing experiences, but you are still a human being and can laugh. Let's just laugh a little together."

In all due modesty, reports from the social workers who follow everything happening to any one patient show that his or her morale "goes through the roof" for a few days after experiencing "the therapy of laughter."

I don't have any "miracles" to report. All patients with whom I have worked have died, but I presume to call this phase of my work a "Ministry of Laughter" because I sense something "spiritual" in reaffirming the humanity of terminally ill patients. Certainly, I feel that it's worth a half hour of my time, anytime.

If God *is*, indeed, "a comedian playing for an audience that's afraid to laugh," then God must want us to laugh. Clinical research is continually emerging that shows we live healthier, longer, certainly *happier* lives if laughter is a significant part of our daily living. In the workshops I present to health-care professionals, pastors, and business groups, I continually urge them "to be a fun person." Be creative, even daring—but always sensitive—in the use of humor; but let *your* sense of humor serve you well in times of stress and encourage others to do the same.

By way of illustration, I usually share one of my favorite examples—the use of humor in some of the memorial services I, as a pastor, have been called upon to lead. At one such service for a beloved scoutmaster who had

died of a heart attack in one of the canoes in which he was leading a troop's camping weekend, I invited those present to share some of the stories of how this dedicated man had touched lives. The night before, while visiting with most of them at the funeral home, I had heard both moving and funny stories about some of the deceased's fifteen years of working with his young scouts, so I knew there were a goodly number of tales. After a few moving accounts of ways he had changed lives, I invited those present to share some of the amusing stories of things that had happened in those meaningful years together. And as the stories came, and laughter filled the sanctuary, there was what can best be described as a "glow" in that room, as a life, now ended, was celebrated in *all* its dimensions.

On a personal note, I can but add that of the many memorial services I have conducted, more people came up after that one than I have ever experienced, saying words to the effect that "Gordon would have loved that."

The therapy of laughter had "struck again!"

Dale L. Anderson MD

Dale L. Anderson, M.D., has been a physician for over thirty-six years and has practiced as a family doctor, a board-certified general surgeon and a board-certified emergency physician His active clinical practice is with the Urgent Care Department of a 450 physician clinic in Minneapolis, MN.

Dr. Anderson is a member of the National Speakers Association and was the 1992-1993 President of the Minnesota Speakers Association and the 1995-1996 President of the Medical Speakers Association. He is one of America's leading health "edu-tainers" and conducts over 100 seminars a year. He coordinates the Minnesota ACT Now! Project, which adapts theater art techniques "that play out 'well' on the health stage"

For seminar and speaking information write Dale L. Anderson, MD, J'ARM, Inc., 2982 W. Owasso Blvd., Roseville, MN 55113

11

Harnessing the Chemistry of Healing

The "ACT Now" Hypothesis

The new field of psychoneuroimmunolgy (PNI) yields insights that can enhance the doctor-patient relationship. One of these is scientific, measurable evidence of the physiological link of emotional states and overall health.

Research over the last two decades reveals the riches of our "pharmacy within." The human body is a vast storehouse of healing chemicals, including many neuropeptides. Endorphins, which are chemically related to morphine, are but one of the PNI neuropeptide families. However, the lay press has labeled all the PNI neuropeptides as "endorphins" and called them the "inner uppers that get us high on life." As a physician, I can more easily discuss the mind-body connection if I borrow from the lay press and speak in lay terms and refer to the healthy neuropeptides simply as "endorphins."

My patients can be told that research shows that a rise in "endorphin" levels is linked to a variety of benefits. Physical benefits include muscle relaxation, appetite suppression, enhanced immune function, and reduced pain and tissue inflammation. Endorphin elevation can bring psychological benefits also, including a sense of euphoria that counters fear, anger, and depression.

Knowing this leads to an exciting possibility. Imagine what would happen if we, my patients, and society knew how to systematically access their positive healing chemistry. They could consistently reduce stress, have positive emotions, and bolster their immunity.

Yet this possibility comes with a troubling question: How do we help my patients and others access positive emotions and the related chemistry of healing?

Drawing on the theater tradition

For an answer to this question, we can turn to a centuries-old tradition, one that thrives in the metropolitan area. I refer to the tradition of the theater.

Actors have a powerful set of techniques for taking on the emotional states of the characters they play. Many of these techniques come from the work of Constantin

Stanislavski, the great director who once headed the Moscow Art Theater and created the "method" school of acting. One of an actor's main tasks is to portray powerful emotions. Ironically, Stanislavski held that feelings are not directly controllable. We cannot choose to feel joy, serenity, or other feelings by sheer wishing. However, we can control many aspects of our actions and thoughts that influence feelings. These include:

- How rapidly and deeply we breathe
- How we sit, stand, or walk
- What we say to ourselves
- What we say to others

- How we speak (including inflection, pitch, and tone of voice)
- How we gesture
- How we place our attention
- What we picture in our minds
- How we costume and groom
- Our facial expression

Stanislavski agreed with psychologist William James, who held that feelings follow action, and emotion follows motion. To use a simple example, we often smile when we feel happy. In addition, we often feel happy when we smile.

Skilled actors know this. They understand that certain postures, motions, and thoughts are associated with certain emotions. Transferring this idea to medicine, physicians too, recognize that patients who positively script, stage, costume, direct and ACT healthy and happy change their chemistry. And often the resulting positive "head" chemistry is a treatment in itself or complements and enhances conventionally prescribed medications.

The "Act Now" hypothesis

These ideas make up the bare bones of a new paradigm for health promotion. This paradigm links the dramatic arts with the medical arts. I call it the "Act Now " hypothesis. Its main points are that:

- Emotions are closely linked to chemical changes in the body.

- Certain emotions seem to promote health, while others seem to impair health.
- We can access more healthful emotional states and healing chemistry by consciously modeling—acting like and thinking like healthy people.

I want to emphasize that this is hypothesis, not fact. Further research is needed to test these ideas. Yet this hypothesis offers possible benefits that we cannot afford to ignore, particularly here in Minnesota. We are recognized as the healthiest metro area in the country, and the Twin Cities is the third largest center of the performing arts. So a coalition of dramatic artists thinking medically and medical arts thinking dramatically could identify and teach stage skills that could be introduced into the theater of health, and each individual can learn how to ACT WELL. I try to explain the Act Now hypothesis to patients in non-technical terms. I say that healthy people know how to "live it up." They know ways to raise their "inner uppers," their endorphins and other healthful chemicals. We often describe these people who have developed the habits of ACTing WELL as optimistic, humorous, creative confident, perceptive, productive, popular, and successful.

If one wants to feel happier then think, speak, move, and gesture like a happy person. In short, take on the role of someone who functions at a high level of physical and mental health. Over time, your thoughts and actions can invite positive emotions—a positive, healthier chemistry.

What physicians can do

The “Act Now” hypothesis comes with an implied program of action. Physicians can direct some dramatic changes in their patients by learning and teaching a few performance techniques.

Endorphin levels are raised through a wide range of activities. Besides laughing, these include smiling, eating, exercising, cheering, singing, listening to music, creative visualizing, etc. Obviously, not all these are appropriate for every occasion; yet, some are, and it pays to capitalize on them.

Actors use many actions and thoughts in the "green room" to access the chemistry for a happy part. The following are just three simple, low-cost strategies you can start using and teaching immediately to "play" a part WELL.

Smile

Smiling can produce an immediate change of physical, mental, and emotional state. Test this idea for yourself: The next time you're feeling sad or mad, force yourself to smile. Do this no matter how silly it seems at the moment. Then carefully observe the resulting changes in your attitude. Notice any subtle feelings of relaxation or relief.

When we smile, we become our own "inner" physician, filling an endorphin prescription from our pharmacy within. If we want to alter our brain chemistry, we can just smile. So, the first, cheapest, and easiest way to start changing your chemistry is to "costume" your face and the faces of those in your "support cast." At first a forced smile will feel "fake" and "unreal," as in any new habit formation, but eventually the act will become "real."

Laugh

Next, see if you can upgrade those smiles into outbursts of outright laughter. For a personal demonstration, I offer a "Laughter RX." Fill it for yourself, and then give it to others. The instructions are simple: Stand in front of a mirror and belly laugh. Do this three times each day for at least fifteen seconds. Do this with real commitment. We're not talking a mere snicker. I'm recommending a full-blown, belly-shaking, thigh-slapping, knee-buckling guffaw.

You might feel silly doing this. Fine; do it anyway. There's a saying: Lead with the body and the mind will follow. In other words, let an action generate the physiology of your emotions. Don't wait to laugh until you feel happy. Laugh, boost your endorphins, and then feel happy.

There are several ways you can use the laughter prescription. First, do it yourself, both at home and at work. Then try it with your family and staff. For sure, they will begin by laughing at you—but eventually with you. Laughter is contagious, infectious and catching. Group laughter is a great tension reliever.

Connect

Many believe it's impossible for human beings to enjoy optimum health unless they experience genuine connection. Here I use the word "connection" in the sense of bonding

with friends, family, lovers, nature, and community. Method actors say that they must be "in touch" with their audiences to create the chemistry of an "on" performance.

A simple handshake, a comforting touch or hug, a smile or laugh all have the power to connect people in ways that are non-threatening. So when ATT (appropriate, timely and tasteful), give the pat on the shoulder and other everyday gestures of friendliness and support.

Of course, there are other ways to foster connection than physical touch. Encourage your staff to spend non-hurried time with each patient. People also appreciate being asked about their homes, families, hobbies, travel plans and social interests. Much of customer service and patient satisfaction boils down to the simple act of asking questions and listening to the answers. These "acts" are the art of medicine, business, *and life*.

There are few better ways to foster the healthy chemistry of happiness than smiling, laughter, and connection. So put on a smile; laugh for the "health of it"; and stay in touch. In doing so, you'll start to harness the chemistry of healing and test the "Act Now!" hypothesis for yourself.

Patty Wooten

Patty Wooten is a woman who knows how to laugh at life. She's a successful nurse, a dynamic speaker and a hilarious clown. Often called "The Queen Mother of Therapeutic Humor", Ms. Wooten has entertained audiences from Modesto to Miami to Madrid. She is a veteran of countless radio shows and has appeared on such TV shows as NBC's Real Life, Home and Family Show, and Good Morning L.A.. Her work has been featured in US Today, Better Homes and Gardens, Psychology Today, and USA Weekend magazine. She is also the author of two best selling books, Heart Humor and Healing and her newest release Compassionate Laughter.

Patty is the perfect choice for keynote presentations, workshops, partner programs, after dinner speeches, custom comedy presentation and clown entertainment. If it's "laughter you're after" call Patty Wooten – she's tickled the funny bones of over 100,000 happy people.

You may contact Patty at:
Jest for the Health of It;
PO Box 8484, Santa Cruz, CA 95061. Phone: 408-460-1600, e-mail:pwooten@jesthealth.com.

Or her web site: http://www.jesthealth.com

12 Laughter and Healing

Laughter serves as a blocking agent. Like a bullet-proof vest, it may help protect you against the ravages of negative emotions that can assault you in disease.

—Norman Cousins

Does a sense of humor help us cope with stressful events in our lives? Can humor and laughter stimulate changes in the body that enhance our health and facilitate recovery from illness? More than a thousand years ago, the Bible advised us, "A merry heart does good like a medicine, but a broken spirit dries the bones." Today, modern scientific research is proving exactly how this happens.

Laughter Research Begins

Dr. William Fry, professor emeritus at Stanford University, began his study of laughter in the early 1960's. He found that laughter is characterized by a pattern of stimulation followed by a period of relaxation. Many muscles are activated when we laugh. A deep belly laugh activates the diaphragm, abdominal, chest, and facial muscles. These muscles then relax after the laughter subsides. This process releases muscle tension, which may explain why people experience a decrease in pain after laughter.

Fry also discovered that the cardiovascular system is also significantly affected during laughter. Heart rate and blood pressure increase in proportion to the intensity and duration of laughter. This increase in cardiac output raises blood flow and enhances the delivery of oxygen, cellular nutrients, and immune components to tissues. (Fry, 1986)

He also measured laughter's effect on the respiratory system. During laughter, we exhale more air than we inhale. This process removes the residual air in the lungs. Residual air contains high concentrations of carbon dioxide and water vapor, which can support the growth of bacteria and promote lung infections. Vigorous laughter helps to remove the trapped air, creating a space for more oxygen to be absorbed into the blood. (Fry, 1971)

Laughter Research Continues

Norman Cousins, journalist and editor of the Saturday Review, used laughter to facilitate his recovery from a degenerative collagen disease. In his book, *Anatomy of an Illness*, he captured the attention of both the medical and lay communities when he discussed the possible health benefits of laughter.

In 1968, Cousins was diagnosed with ankylosing spondylitis, a potentially life-threatening, degenerative disease of the collagen tissue. Collagen is a substance in the connective tissue of the body which is essential in holding the cells and larger structures of the body together. Cousins' case was so extreme that he soon experienced great difficulty and pain moving his joints. He was told that his prospect for recovery was very bleak. Because of discomfort and fatigue, he was unable to travel or play tennis, activities which brought him great joy and satisfaction.

Cousins refused to accept his grim prognosis and decided to take charge of his own treatment, working in partnership with his physician. He remembered reading about the adverse consequences of negative emotional states on the chemical balance of the body.

He reasoned that, if negative emotions played any part in predisposing him to illness, then perhaps positive emotions would aid in his recovery. He sought activities that increased his positive emotions, such as faith, hope, festivity, determination, confidence, joy, and a strong will to live.

> *Each human being possesses a beautiful system for fighting disease. This system provides the body with cancer-fighting cells–cells that can crush cancer cells or poison them one by one with the body's own chemotherapy. This system works better when the patient is relatively free of depression, which is what a strong will to live and a blazing determination can help to do. When we add these inner resources to the resources of medical science, we're reaching out for the best.*
>
> *—Norman Cousins*

Cousins knew that laughter helped create these positive emotions. With this in mind, Cousins watched films of the Marx Brothers and *Candid Camera*. He had nurses read to him from humorous books. He played practical jokes and told jokes. And, lo and behold, he began feeling better. Blood tests showed that his sedimentation rate (an index of the degree of infection or inflammation in the body) decreased after his laughter sessions and continued to fall as he gradually recovered.

After several months of this "humor therapy," his illness resolved and never bothered him again. One could argue that Cousins would have recovered anyway, even without the laughter. Or one could say that the results were not scientifically significant and represent the observations of a single case. However, Cousins continued his quest to understand just how his healing occurred. Cousins spent the remaining twelve years of his life as an Adjunct Professor at UCLA Medical School where he established a "Humor Task Force" to coordinate and support clinical research on laughter. He reported some early research results in his second book, *Head First: The Biology of Hope* (Cousins, 1989). Today, 25 years after Cousins' self-healing experience with laughter, we have the scientific research to explain the specific physiological changes which his individual story suggested.

Laughter Research at Loma Linda University

Doctors Lee Berk and Stanley Tan have completed research showing that the immune system is stimulated and strengthened during the experience of mirthful laughter (Berk & Tan, 1989b). In a carefully controlled study, they examined the immune response of medical students who viewed a video performance of the comedian Gallager, the "Vegomatic Man." Blood samples were analyzed before, during, and after the comedy routine. A control group that did not experience the humorous intervention was used for comparison.

In an interview with Dr. Berk, he discussed how his research explains the connection between humor and laughter and our health. "Essentially, we found that mirthful laughter serves to modulate specific immune system components. By modulate, we mean that chemicals released during the emotional experience of mirth can connect to receptors on the surface of the immune cells. This connection stimulates a change in the molecular machinery inside the cells. Specific molecules known as immunoregulators are like plugs that fit into receptors and subsequently increase or decrease the immune cell activity. One metaphor for modulation of immune activity is the conductor of an orchestra. Although the conductor does not actually play an instrument, he influences the tempo, harmony and volume of the music produced by the orchestra. Mirthful laughter would be like the conductor who enhances sonic integration and brings out melodious harmony. Whereas distressful emotions would be like the conductor who brings out harsh disharmonious sounds. Emotions, like a conductor, modulates the activity and effectiveness of the immune cells, although it does not directly protect the body from insult or infection."

This research team also recorded increased activity in natural killer cells in the participants' response to laughter (Berk & Tan, 1989a). Natural killer cells release a substance that destroys tumor cells and deadly viruses. Among cancer patients, reduced natural-killer-cell activity is associated with an increase in the spread of tumors (Levy, 1985).

"Our findings," Berk explained, "revealed that serum cortisol levels decreased significantly in the group experiencing laughter. Cortisol levels are known to increase during the experience of stress emotions, when the brain signals the adrenal gland to product corticosteroids. These chemicals will increase blood sugar and decrease the immune response. Berk and Tan's findings support the hypotheses that laughter keeps our immune system strong, which in turn keeps us healthy.

We found that for the experimental group – those exposed to the humorous film, there was an increase in the number of activated T-cells

(T lymphocytes). Apparently during mirthful laughter, there is a chemical stimulus that tells these lymphocytes to become active, to get prepared for combat with a potential virus, bacteria or foreign protein."

Dr. Berk continued, "We also saw an increase in the numbers of natural killer cells (NK cells) which are very important for immune surveillance. Natural killer cells are a type of immune cell that attack viral infected cells and some types of cancer or tumor cells. Natural killer cells do not appear to need prior sensitization or communication to be activated. They know and recognize when another cell is aberrant or infected. Every day, cells in our body undergo a lot of change, creating potential carcinogenic cells. Fortunately, when our immune system is functioning properly, the natural killer cells destroy and kill aberrant cells. Natural killer cells are significant in terms of immunosurveillance. Our research shows that not only the activity of the natural killer cells increase during mirthful laughter, but the actual number of natural killer cells increases as well.

Our studies also revealed an increase in the antibody-immunoglobulin A (IgA). IgA is an immunoglobulin that resides, in part, in the mucousal areas. It helps us fight upper respiratory tract insults and infections. We also saw an increase in the number of B cells (B lymphocytes) which goes along with the immunoglobulins increasing. In addition, we found an increase in a substance called

Complement 3. The substance helps the antibodies pierce the cell open when the cell is dysfunctional or infected and needs to be disrupted or broken. Complement 3 was found to be increased both during recovery and the next day.

Our most recent research was presented at the Psychoneuroimmunology Research Society meeting in April, 1996. We found significant increases in gama interferon (IFN). The precise role of IFN in human diseases and therapy is not completely understood. However, we know that it is clearly involved in the defense against parasites, viruses and possible tumor cells. A deficiency in the production of gama interferon has been related to persistent viral infections. Our studies showed that increased gammainterferon levels not only increased during the humor intervention, but also lasted into recovery and through the next day. It should be noted that plasma volume, hematocrit and total serum protein showed
no significant change over these time points. It is well known that interferon plays important roles in the growth and differentiation of cytotoxic T cells, activation of natural killer cells and functions as B-cell maturation factor. Based upon this understanding, it is reasonable to propose that there indeed may be a correlative relationship at a molecular level between the presence of gamma interferon and other components of the immune system."

The Mind/Body Connection

Research has also shown that a strong sense of humor can balance our negative mood shifts when events force us to change (Lefcourt, 1986). Different emotions stimulate a variety of chemical secretions from our brains. These chemicals (neurotransmitters) carry messages to the immune cells and can cause the cells to change their behavior and ability to protect us from disease. (Pert, 1985,1986)

These research results help us understand the mind-body connections. The emotions and moods we experience directly effect our immune system. A sense of humor allows us to perceive and appreciate the incongruities of life and provides moments of joy and delight. These positive emotions can create neurochemical changes within our bodies that will buffer the immunosuppressive effects of stress.

Humor and laughter have therapeutic benefits, and science offers proof that we should "Jest for the Health of It."

Bibliography

Berk, L.S., Tan, S.A., et al. "Eustress of Mirthful Laughter Modifies Natural Killer Cell Activity." *Clinical Research*. (37), 1989a, 115A.
Berk, Lee & Tan, Stanley. "Neuroendocrine and Stress Hormone Changes During Mirthful Laughter." *American Journal of the Medical Sciences*. 1989b, (298) 390-396.
Berk, L., Tan,S., and Fry, W. "Eustress of Humor Associated Laughter Modulates Specific Immune System Components" Annals of Behavior Medicine, Vol. 15, 1993 Supplement, p.S111
Berk, L. And Tan, S. "A Positive Emotion the Eustress of Mirthful Laughter

Modulates the Immune System Lymphokine Interferon-Gamma" Psychoneuroimmunolgy Research Society Annual Meetings. Abstract Supplement, April 17-20, 1995, A.1-A.4
Cousins, Norman. *Anatomy of an Illness*. New York: W. W. Norton, 1979.
Cousins, Norman. *Head First: the Biology of Hope*. New York: Dutton, 1989.
Fry, William. "Mirth and Oxygen Saturation of Peripheral Blood." Psychotherapy and Psychosomatics, (19), 1971, 76-84.
Fry, William. "Humor, Physiology and the Aging Process." In Nahemow, Lucille, (Ed.) Humor and Aging. Orlando, FL: Academic Press, 1986, 81-98.
Lefcourt, Herbert & Martin, Rod. Humor and Life Stress: Antidote to Adversity. New York: Springer-Verlag, 1986.
Lefcourt, Herbert, et al. "Humor and Immune System Function." International Journal of Humor Research. (3), 1990, 305-321.
Martin, Rod, et.al. "Sens of humor, hassles, and immunoglobulin A: Evidence for the stress-moderating effect of humor". Int'l Psychiatry in Medicine. 1985;18 (2):pp 93-105
McGhee, Paul *The Laughter Remedy* Dubuque, IA: Kendall-Hunt Pub, 1996
Pert, Candace, et al. "Neuropeptides and their Receptors: A Psychosomatic Network." Journal of Immunology. (135), 1985, 820s-826s.
Pert, Candace *Molecules of Emotion* New York: Schribner Publishing, 1997
Wooten, Patty, *Compassionate Laughter.* Salt Lake City: Commune-a-key, 1996
Wooten, Patty, "Humor – Antidote for Stress". Holistic Nursing Practice. 10(2), 1996, pp.49-55.

Books and Products from Patty Wooten

Jest for You, PO Box 8484, Santa Cruz, CA 95060
408-460-1600

Compassionate Laugher by Patty Wooten	$13.00
Heart, Humor and Healing by Patty Wooten	$10.00
Tales from the Bedside Vol. 2 by John Wise	$13.00
Perils of Nancy Nurse Video (40 min)	$25.00
Laughs! Jest for Health Video (36 min)	$25.00
Mental Floss	$ 4.00
Wiper Glasses (battery operated)	$ 7.00
Groucho Glasses (windup)	$ 5.00
Pacifier	$ 3.00
Foam Granite Rock	$ 3.00
Squeezable Stress Doll	$ 7.00
Squeeking Hammer	$ 3.00
Magic Wand	$ 2.00
All Hats	$10.00
Smile on a Stick	$ 2.00
Mirth Aid Kit (empty box)	$ 8.00
Clown Nose – Red Foam	$ 1.00
Boxing Nun Puppet	$10.00

California Residents Add 7.5% tax
Sipping Charge for <u>ANY</u> size order $ 3.00